KV-179-278

Responsible Tourism

ISSUES

Volume 109

Editor

Craig Donnellan

Independence

Educational Publishers

Cambridge

First published by Independence
PO Box 295
Cambridge CB1 3XP
England

British Library Cataloguing in Publication Data
Reponsible Tourism – (Issues Series)
I. Donnellan, Craig II. Series
338.4'791

ISBN 1 86168 329 4

Printed in Great Britain
MWL Print Group Ltd

Typeset by
Lisa Firth

Cover
The illustration on the front cover is by
Simon Kneebone.

CONTENTS

Chapter One: Tourism Issues

Chapter Two: Responsible Tourism

Introduction

Responsible Tourism is the one hundred and ninth volume in the **Issues** series. The aim of this series is to offer up-to-date information about important issues in our world.

Responsible Tourism looks at contemporary tourism issues and different forms of reponsible tourism such as sustainable, community and eco-tourism.

The information comes from a wide variety of sources and includes:
Government reports and statistics
Newspaper reports and features
Magazine articles and surveys
Website material
Literature from lobby groups
and charitable organisations.

It is hoped that, as you read about the many aspects of the issues explored in this book, you will critically evaluate the information presented. It is important that you decide whether you are being presented with facts or opinions. Does the writer give a biased or an unbiased report? If an opinion is being expressed, do you agree with the writer?

Responsible Tourism offers a useful starting-point for those who need convenient access to information about the many issues involved. However, it is only a starting-point. At the back of the book is a list of organisations which you may want to contact for further information.

*****

Global tourism: growing fast

Tourism is the world's largest industry, with an annual revenue of almost $500 billion. And it is growing fast, with airline arrivals expected to double by 2010

Leisure is estimated to account for 75 per cent of all international travel. The World Tourism Organisation (WTO) estimated there were 694 million international tourist arrivals in 2003, a drop of 1.2 per cent (attributed to the problems of the Iraq conflict, SARS and a generally weak world economy). Arrivals have picked up in 2004, and they are expected to reach 1.6 billion by 2020. Domestic tourism (people going on holiday in their own country) is generally thought to be 4-5 times greater than international arrivals. The WTO puts global revenue from tourism in 2003 at US$514.4 billion.

Globally, tourism accounts for roughly 35 per cent of exports of services and over 8 per cent of exports of goods (WTO). Tourism is now the world's largest employer. In 2001, the International Labour Organisation (ILO) estimated that globally over 207 million jobs were directly or indirectly employed in tourism. In the UK alone, 10 per cent of total employment is in the tourism sector.

The World Travel and Tourism Council (WTTC) predicts that the ten new accession countries which joined the EU in 2004 will generate up to US$54.6 billion of travel and tourism GDP, and create an extra 3 million jobs. These figures would arguably make tourism the EU's largest business in terms of income.

- For 83 per cent of countries in the world, tourism is one of the top five sources of foreign exchange.
- Caribbean countries derive half their GDP from tourism (World Resources Institute).
- Benidorm's tourism industry accounts for 1 per cent of Spain's GDP.

Where tourists go

Three-quarters of all international travellers visit a country in either Europe or North America. However, the share of international tourists travelling to Asia and the Pacific rose from just 1 per cent in 1950 to 17.2 per cent in 2003. Despite the impact of SARS, which caused an estimated decline of 9.3 per cent in arrivals in 2003, Asia has outstripped the Americas in terms of international tourist arrivals, and is the most popular destination after Europe. China is expected to unseat France as the most visited country and to become the fourth largest source of tourists.

Where tourists come from

Over 80 per cent of international tourists come from just 20 countries in the North – 17 in Europe plus the USA, Canada and Japan. Five nations (the US, Japan, Germany, France and the UK) account for almost half of all tourist spending. Around 15 per cent of tourists originate in East Asia and the Pacific and 5 per cent in Africa, the Middle East, and South Asia combined.

Just over half of all spending on tourism is spent by travellers from just ten countries.

For 83 per cent of countries in the world, tourism is one of the top five sources of foreign exchange

---

The top 15 tourism markets (the above six plus the Netherlands, Canada, China, Austria, Belgium, Sweden, Switzerland, Hong Kong (China) and the Republic of Korea) combined accounted for 70.3 per cent of all tourist spending.

Industry organisations

- World Travel and Tourism Council (WTTC): A trade association based in Brussels and London and made up of around 70 chief executives of major airlines, hotel chains, cruise lines and catering companies.
- World Tourism Organisation (WTO): Based in Madrid and created by the United Nations, the WTO consists of a mix of 130-plus governments and 350 affiliated private enterprises. Compiles industry statistics and market trends.
- American Society of Travel Agents (ASTA): The largest travel trade association in the world, representing 26,500 travel agents in 170 countries (Honey).
- Association of British Travel Agents (ABTA): The trade association of the major British tour operators.

The air industry

Like much of the tourism and travel industry in 2003, air traffic was down an estimated 1 per cent by the end of the year (WTO). Domestic traffic increased by 0.7 per cent, but international traffic fell by 5.5 per cent. These results were heavily influenced by a drop of nearly 11 per cent in traffic to destinations in Asia and the Pacific (attributed mostly to SARS), plus there was a 6.5 per cent drop on Atlantic routes. Trends are picking up again significantly, with the International Air Transport Association (IATA) reporting substantial growth since July 2003, with overall growth of 18 per cent in total passenger traffic. Nevertheless, the substantial hike in fuel prices means that many airlines continue to function at a loss. Most major international airlines are now linked into four global alliances: Oneworld, Star, Sky Team and Qualiflyer.

Growth of tourism

International tourist arrivals increased from 25 million in 1950 to 693 million in 2003, and are predicted to grow to 1.56 billion by 2020 (WTO). Globally, the tourism industry is growing at 4.6 per cent (WTTC). The number of air passengers rose from 9 million in 1945

to 88 million in 1972, 344 million in 1994 and 1.72 billion in 2002 (IATA).

Factors in tourism's growth include:
- **Increasing leisure time:** In 1936, the International Labour Organization convention provided for one week's leave per year for workers in developed countries. In 1970, this was expanded to three weeks, and in 1999 to four weeks.
- **Increased disposable income:** Spending on leisure in the UK has risen from 9 per cent of household income in 1978 to 17 per cent in 1998 (Tearfund: Tourism: An Ethical Issue, 2000). In 2002-3 the UK Family Expenditure Survey found UK households spent £660 a year on holidays, totalling £308 million for the year.
- **Falling real cost of air travel:** Between 1978 and 1998, the real cost of air travel fell by 35 per cent (Air Travel Association). A thousand miles of air travel now requires 61 hours' less work than it did a generation ago.

Growth of tourism to the South

In 1950, 97 per cent of international tourists went to Europe or North America (in fact, to just 15 countries). By 2003 this had fallen to 78.8 per cent. In the mid-1970s, 8 per cent of all international tourists were from the North visiting the South. By the mid-1990s, this had risen to 20 per cent (Honey). In 1999, more than 70 countries received over a million international tourist arrivals.

Growth of tourism in/from the South

In recent years, domestic and intra-regional tourism in the South has grown rapidly, especially in emerging economies such as China, Thailand, India, Korea, and Mexico.
- Tourists originating in Asia and the Pacific increased from 81.8 million in 1995 to 131.2 million in 2002, a total of 18.7 per cent of the world total, and increase of 7.9 per cent since 2001 (WTO).
- In 1995, 108 million people worked in tourism in China and South Asia, compared to only 42 million in the North (North

America, Australasia, Japan and the European Community).
- Intra-regional tourism (people travelling within the same continent/region) accounted for 73 per cent of total tourist arrivals in East Asia and the Pacific in 1998. In Africa, intra-regional tourism increased from 38 per cent of all arrivals in 1980 to 60 per cent in 1990 (WTO).

International tourist arrivals increased from 25 million in 1950 to 693 million in 2003, and are predicted to grow to 1.56 billion by 2020

- 90 per cent of visitors to national parks in Thailand, India and South Africa are domestic tourists (Ceballos-Lascurain 1996). Of 200,000 annual visitors to Kinabalu National Park in Sabah, Malaysia, 90 per cent are Malaysian. At Mt Bromo in Java, Indonesia, 70 per cent of visitors are Indonesian.

This information was compiled by Mark Mann, author of *The Gringo Trail* and Tourism Concern's *Community Tourism Guide* and updated by Francisca Kellett.

- The above information is reprinted with kind permission from Planet 21, an independent charity providing a well-illustrated educational website on sixteen key themes linking people and the environment – for more information please visit www.peopleandplanet.net or see page 41 for their address details.

© Planet 21 2004

Global tourism: growing fast – the statistics

International tourist arrivals, millions (WTO)

Country	2003	% change	% of tourism market
Africa	30.5	+4.9%	4.4%
Americas	112.4	-2.1%	16.2%
Asia and the Pacific	119.1	-9.3%	17.2%
Europe	401.5	+0.4%	57.8%
Middle East	30.4	+10.3%	4.4%
World	*694*	*-1.2%*	

Source: World Tourism Organization (WTO)

Top 10 tourist destinations (international tourist arrivals in millions)

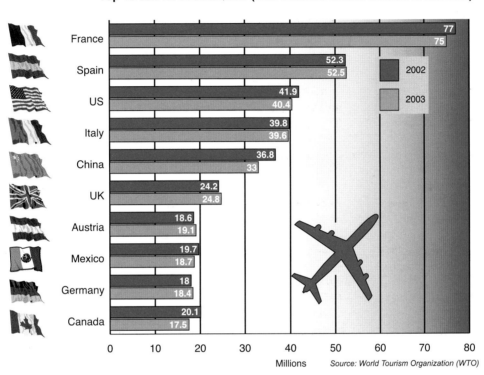

Country	2002	2003
France	77	75
Spain	52.3	52.5
US	41.9	40.4
Italy	39.8	39.6
China	36.8	33
UK	24.2	24.8
Austria	18.6	19.1
Mexico	19.7	18.7
Germany	18	18.4
Canada	20.1	17.5

Millions *Source: World Tourism Organization (WTO)*

Tourists by originating region, millions

Country	Tourists (millions)
Africa	16.8
Americas	120.2
Asia and the Pacific	131.2
Europe	404.9
Middle East	16
Others/unrecorded	13.5

Source: World Tourism Organization (WTO)

Growth of actual passenger traffic (% July 2003 – 2004)

Country	Growth (per cent)
Africa	12.4
Asia and the Pacific	27.7
Europe	11.5
Middle East	21.8
North America	16.2
South America	13

Source: International Air Transport Association (ATTA)

Tourism expenditure by country: top ten tourism markets, 2002

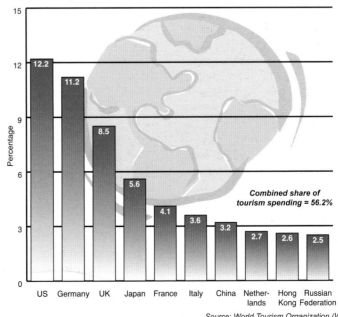

Country	Percentage
US	12.2
Germany	11.2
UK	8.5
Japan	5.6
France	4.1
Italy	3.6
China	3.2
Netherlands	2.7
Hong Kong	2.6
Russian Federation	2.5

Combined share of tourism spending = 56.2%

Source: World Tourism Organization (WTO)

International travel increases

Travel trends 2003: UK residents' visits abroad

In 2003, UK residents made a record 61.4 million visits abroad, up by 3 per cent on the number of visits made in 2002. They spent a record £28.6 billion on these visits, £1.6 billion (6 per cent) more than in 2002.

Purpose of visit

Going on holiday was the most popular reason for UK residents to go abroad. In 2003, two-thirds of visits made by UK residents were to go on holiday, with a record 41.2 million holidays taken. About half (47 per cent) of these were package holidays. Over the five-year period from 1999 to 2003, holidays showed very strong growth, increasing by an average of over 4 per cent each year.

Business trips and visits to friends or relatives were the next most popular reasons for going abroad. In 2003, UK residents made 7.9 million business trips and 8.5 million visits to friends or relatives abroad. The number of business trips peaked in 2000 and has fallen every year since then. Most of the fall in business trips occurred between 2000 and 2001 (a fall of over 7 per cent) and although the number of such visits continued to fall in 2002 and 2003, it was at a slower rate (2 per cent). Visits to friends or relatives have continued to rise between 1999 and 2003.

Visits for miscellaneous reasons (such as shopping, study and medical visits) made by UK residents abroad fell by 11 per cent in 2001 and by 4 per cent in 2002, but rose by 8 per cent in 2003. As a result, UK residents made 3.8 million miscellaneous visits abroad in 2003, 7 per cent fewer than in 1999.

> *In 2003, two-thirds of visits made by UK residents were to go on holiday, with a record 41.2 million holidays taken*

Country of visit

Almost three-quarters (73 per cent) of all visits abroad made by UK residents were to EU Europe and these accounted for 57 per cent of all spending overseas (£16.3 billion). In contrast, only 7 per cent of UK residents' visits abroad were to North America but these accounted for 13 per cent of total spending overseas. While visits to all other regions of the world generally increased every year in the five years since 1999,

trips to North America increased until 2000 and have declined every year since then.

Spain and France were the most popular countries visited by UK residents, with 13.8 million and 12.0 million visits each (respectively). Together, these two countries accounted for 42 per cent of all visits abroad. As in previous years, nine out of the ten most popular countries UK residents visited in 2003 were in EU Europe. The exception was the USA.

Although the majority of spending overseas by UK residents occurred in EU Europe, the average spend on a trip to North America and Non EU Europe was higher. The average spend per visit was highest in 'Other Countries' (£908) and North America (£886) and was lowest in EU Europe (£361). In part, this reflected the longer stays involved with visits to North America and 'Other Countries'.

In terms of the countries visited in 2003, UK residents spent the most in Spain (£5.8 billion), followed by France (£3.7 billion) and the USA (£3.3 billion)

Gateways to and from the UK

Air travel was the most popular mode of travel for both UK residents travelling abroad and for overseas

residents visiting the UK. In 2003, UK residents made a record 47.1 million visits by air, representing over three-quarters (77 per cent) of all visits abroad. Overseas residents made 17.6 million visits to the UK by air (71 per cent of all visits to the UK).

Overall, Channel Tunnel visits accounted for 8 per cent of UK residents' visits abroad and 11 per cent of overseas visits to the UK. Visits by sea accounted for the remaining 15 per cent of UK residents' visits abroad and 18 per cent of overseas residents' visits to the UK.

The mode of transport and gateway used varied according to where people were travelling to or from. In general, Heathrow continued to be the most popular gateway for visits to and from the UK. It was the most popular gateway for overseas visitors from every region of the world and 34 per cent of all overseas residents visiting the UK entered through Heathrow. Heathrow also accounted for nearly a fifth (18 per cent) of all visits overseas by UK residents.

Visits to destinations outside EU Europe by UK residents were almost entirely made by air whereas almost a third of visits to EU Europe were made by sea or via the Tunnel. Nearly two-fifths of visits to the UK made by residents of EU Europe were by sea or Channel Tunnel.

Balance of payments

Since 1986, the spending by UK residents on visits abroad was higher than spending by overseas residents visiting the UK. This deficit has continued to increase to a record of £16.7 billion in 2003. This was £1.5 billion more than the deficit in 2002.

■ The above information is an extract from a press release provided by the Office of National Statistics – please visit their website at the URL www.statistics.gov.uk to view the full text or for more information, or if you wish to write to them please see page 41 for their address details.

© Crown Copyright 2004

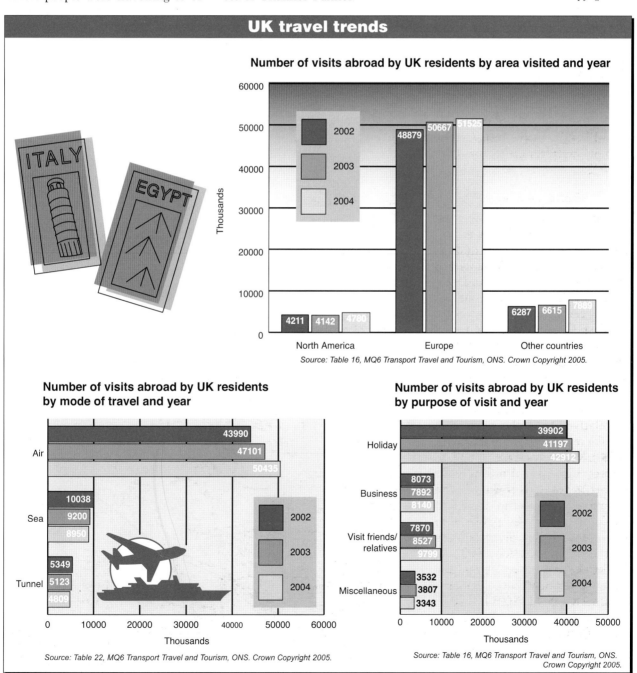

UK travel trends

Number of visits abroad by UK residents by area visited and year

Source: Table 16, MQ6 Transport Travel and Tourism, ONS. Crown Copyright 2005.

Number of visits abroad by UK residents by mode of travel and year

Source: Table 22, MQ6 Transport Travel and Tourism, ONS. Crown Copyright 2005.

Number of visits abroad by UK residents by purpose of visit and year

Source: Table 16, MQ6 Transport Travel and Tourism, ONS. Crown Copyright 2005.

UK tourism at all-time high

Latest visitor figures show further increase on record-breaking year

Inbound tourism figures for the first two months of 2005 have given a solid start to the new year with 4 million visits made to the UK by overseas residents – an eleven per cent increase on January and February 2004 – VisitBritain said today (8 April 2005). The increases in spending and visits follow a record-breaking year in 2004 when nearly 28 million international visitors spent £13 billion in the UK.

During January and February, the fastest growth rates came from markets outside of Western Europe and North America. Visits from the Rest of World region are up 17 per cent on 2004 (780,000), while Western European visits rose 13 per cent to 2.7 million. The provisional data also indicates that the £1.6 billion spent by overseas visitors in the first two months of the year is up 11 per cent on 2004.

Tom Wright, VisitBritain chief executive, said: 'This is a very positive start to the new year and good news for Britain's tourism industry as we continue to grow the value of the industry towards £100 billion by 2010. However, changing patterns in the landscape of global tourism mean that there is growing potential for increasing visits and spending from developing markets in Eastern Europe, South-East Asia and China, as well as continuing to support traditional ones such as France, Germany and Ireland.'

VisitBritain is increasing its focus and investment in new and developing 'growth' markets to the benefit of all parts of Britain. Travel trade, media and PR strategies, coupled to website development and contact centre activities in the Czech Republic, Greece, Hungary, Malaysia and Thailand, follow similar activity already undertaken in China, Poland, Russia and South Korea.

Since April 2005, Scotland, Wales, London and England have been taking more of a lead in marketing their respective destinations in France, Germany, Ireland and the Netherlands. VisitBritain will continue to offer a range of core services through its offices in these countries and the national tourist boards will be able to add value to the delivery of their marketing activities through a menu of additional services. VisitBritain's England Marketing division will co-ordinate and lead the marketing of England in these international markets, working in close partnership with the English regions and destinations.

■ The above information is from VisitBritain's website which can be found at www.visitbritain.com

© VisitBritain 2005

Tourism is changing

The industry must move into the 21st century – Jowell

Tessa Jowell today (16 March 2005) urged the tourism industry to meet the needs of 21st-century, web-based consumers by getting behind EnglandNet – a new £10 million online one-stop shop for holidaymakers in England.

From May, EnglandNet will, for the first time, offer holidaymakers all the information they need to know about a destination in England at the click of a mouse. It rationalises the often bewildering array of websites travellers have to navigate to find accommodation and travel information.

Speaking at the first National Tourism conference in London, the Culture Secretary stressed to industry leaders the need to recognise the importance of the Internet travel industry – 60 per cent of travellers now book online.

Tessa Jowell said: 'The Internet enables us all to be travel agents. Consumers increasingly demand a tailor-made holiday and they want to know they're going to get a quality product before they've left the comfort of home.

'EnglandNet will deliver just that. It will provide a much needed shop window for what the UK has to offer. It will be equally accessible whether the traveller lives in Charlton or China.'

EnglandNet will:

■ increase choice – giving travellers an online menu to choose from before they've even left home;
■ drive up standards – people will know whether they are booking a quality product; and
■ boost business – helping towards the goal of making tourism a £100bn-a-year industry by 2010.

Tom Wright, Chief Executive of VisitBritain, said: 'The EnglandNet project will ensure England's online presence remains ahead of rival destinations and provide thousands of our tourism businesses with a strong competitive advantage in the huge global travel market.

'Every part of the industry – from accommodation providers, tour operators and travel agents, to attractions, events, tourist boards and individual destinations – will benefit from EnglandNet as it will better connect millions more potential visitors to a greater variety of England's tourism products and services.'

■ The above information is from the Department of Culture, Media and Sport's website which can be found at www.culture.gov.uk

© Crown Copyright 2005

Major boost for world tourism

International tourism obtains its best results in 20 years

After three years of stagnant growth, international tourism experienced a spectacular rebound in 2004. According to WTO World Tourism Barometer, presented to the media at a news conference in Bangkok, Thailand, international tourist arrivals reached an all-time record of 760 million – an increase of 10% over 2003.

The main purpose of the press conference was to present the Phuket Action Plan, adopted on 1 February 2005 by WTO's Executive Council at its special session in Kata Beach, Phuket. The Plan is aimed at accelerating tourism recovery in the Indian Ocean to ensure that the tourism sector in the afflicted countries emerges from the tsunami disaster stronger and more resilient than ever before. Last year's record results for Asia and the Pacific should go a long way to contributing to a rapid recovery.

Growth was common to all regions, but was predominantly strong in Asia and the Pacific (+29%) and in the Middle East (+20%). Double-digit growth was also registered in the Americas (+10%), while Africa (+7%) and Europe (+4%) performed below the world average, but still substantially improved their results of previous years. 2004 was marked by the strong rebound of Asia and the Pacific after the setbacks suffered in 2003 under the blow of SARS, by the return of the Americas to positive results and by the redistribution of overall tourism flows in Europe and in the Americas under the effects of the USD/euro exchange rate. The recovery of the world economy, and in particular of the economies of important American and European generating markets, strongly contributed to the very good results obtained in 2004. The fears of the impact of the oil prices were overall offset as the year went by and such increases were being absorbed by the dynamism of the world economy and seem to have not affected the consumers' travel confidence.

'As we foresaw in October, tourism in 2004 reached a record of 760 million international tourist arrivals and the best growth rate of the last 20 years,' WTO Secretary-General Francesco Frangialli said. 'We are confident that the tourism sector is back on the right track after three difficult years and though still in commotion over the tragic events in Asia, the tourism sector will surely show again its extraordinary resilience and its ability to overcome difficulties by making an important contribution to the quick recovery of the affected countries'.

In a context of double-digit world tourism revival, Europe reports the lowest result of all regions. International tourist arrivals grew by 4% to a total of 414 million, driven in particular by the excellent performance of countries in Central and Eastern Europe (+8%) and in Northern Europe (+7%). In contrast, results were significantly more modest in Southern/Mediterranean Europe (+3%) and in Western Europe (+2%). The more mature destinations in the euro zone were particularly affected by the increased competition from non-euro destinations, not only in Europe, but also in North Africa (Morocco and Tunisia) and in the Middle East (Egypt).

2004 was definitely the year of full recovery in Asia and the Pacific as the region attained a 29% growth rate, receiving an estimated volume of 154 million tourist arrivals. Following the trend already seen during the last months of 2003, most of the destinations in North-East and South-East Asia rebounded very strongly from the SARS effects, leading both subregions to end the year with a projected increase of around 30%.

After three years of depressed figures, 2004 was the year that finally brought tourism in the Americas back to the growth side. Though still lagging behind the 2000 record volume of 128 million arrivals, international tourist arrivals increased by an exceptional 10% in 2004 to a total of 124 million, as all subregions performed positively.

Argentina's improving economic situation, together with the devaluation of the peso, contributed to the good results obtained by the country (+11% in the first three quarters of the year), but also to the positive performance of nearby countries such as Uruguay (+28% until November), Chile (+14% up to October) and Paraguay (+15% for the full year) due to its importance as traffic generator in these destinations.

In Africa (+7%), 2004 was a particularly buoyant year for destinations in North Africa, which with a 17% increase rate contributed determinately to the overall growth registered in the region, as performance of sub-Saharan destinations was rather flat (+1%).

In the Middle East tourism continues to be one of the most dynamic economic sectors. Arrivals grew by an estimated 20% to a total of 35 million, which makes the region the fourth most visited in the world, surpassing for the first time the volume of Africa (estimated to have received 33 million arrivals in 2004).

■ The above information is from the World Tourism Organization's website which can be found at www.world-tourism.org, or see page 41 for their address details.

© WTO 2005

Independent holidays

British pack in traditional package holiday

With the summer holidays now a distant memory and the dark nights setting in, latest research from Mintel shows that the quintessentially English holidaymaker is facing extinction. Not only has the archetypal package holiday lost out to the more modern independently-booked trip, British adults now look for more than simply egg, chips and a pint in front of the football.

Some 40% of those who had been on an independently booked holiday had arranged it on the Internet compared to fewer than three in ten (27%) who had used a travel agent

While 'a place to relax and unwind' (61%) is the number-one priority, it turns out that the typical British tourist is in fact more of a 'culture vulture' than we are often led to believe. Indeed, 'an interesting landscape' (42%), 'experiencing a different culture' and 'cities, heritage or architecture to see' (both 40%) make up the top three wishes, following 'a place to relax and unwind'. These preferences are some way ahead of 'a beach or pool' (36%) and considerably more important than 'good shopping' (14%), 'familiar food' (13%) or having 'other Brits around' (7%).

'British holidaymakers have in the past received bad press and are often portrayed as simply wanting to live their British lifestyles in a warmer country when they go abroad. But this research shows that Brits abroad do want more from their holiday and many clearly do take an interest in the country they are visiting as well as the local people and culture,' comments Silvia Bartels, senior leisure analyst at Mintel.

British are doing it for themselves

This year we will book some 24 million independent holidays, which equates to 55% of the holiday bookings market. This is up from fewer than 22 million just last year. Between 1998 and 2004 the number of independently booked holidays has risen by an impressive 60%, but what is even more astounding is that the expenditure on these holidays has more than doubled over the same period from a little over £5.5 billion in 1998 to an estimated £11.7 billion this year.

'The increased popularity of the independent holiday owes almost everything to the Internet. Essentially the Internet has brought the travel agent to most people's sitting rooms and it can no longer be argued that booking a package holiday is necessarily more convenient, as the greater use of the Internet has simplified the process for the independent traveller. Low cost airlines have also helped, especially as three-quarters of all independent holidays are taken from the UK by air,' explains Silvia Bartels.

Exclusive consumer research carried out for Mintel also supports this, as almost two in four (38%) adults had booked a holiday independently in the last year, compared to just one in four (25%) who had booked a package holiday. What is more, the popularity of independent holidays is expected to continue to increase further, with expenditure on these holidays forecast to rise by a massive 78%, to reach a value of just over £21 billion by 2009.

ABTA (the Association of British Travel Agents) confirms that these changes are already having a significant impact on the travel industry. 'These predictions for independent travel are impressive and underline the reason why our members are adapting quickly to offer very flexible booking arrangements for those customers who want to remain relatively independent,' comments Keith Betton, Head of Corporate Affairs for ABTA.

British holidaymakers easy to please

Surprisingly, when it comes to enticing those Brits to book independently, British travellers have simple demands. More appealing than discounts on the hotel or car hire, freebies or vouchers is the option to stay in the hotel room until it is time to leave or at least have a late check-out time.

'Convenience is obviously very important to British holidaymakers and in many cases it is more

important than saving money. Having spent time unwinding away from home, it seems that when it comes to heading back to the UK, many want to keep things as simple and stress-free as possible,' comments Silvia Bartels.

Internet is the key

Some 40% of those who had been on an independently-booked holiday had arranged it on the Internet compared to fewer than three in ten (27%) who had used a travel agent. Interestingly men (31%) are far more likely than women (24%) to use a travel agent.

'Most significantly, the Internet was used by independent holiday-makers more often than any other method when purchasing the holiday. As there is a clear connection between independent holidays and short breaks, it is likely that a large proportion of these consumers accessed the low cost airline websites, or even one of the more popular third parties for travel, such as www.lastminute.com, expedia.co.uk or travelocity.co.uk or scheduled airline websites such as British Airways,' comments Silvia Bartels.

The Internet will continue to play a large part in the distribution chain of all holidays, but in particular independent holidays. Consumers are certainly becoming more confident in booking their transport and accommodation separately.

The new seekers

Adventure travel was once the preserve of backpackers. Not any more. Chris Moss on the rise of the intrepid holidaymaker

Which would you rather come back with from holiday – a tan or tales of how you learned to cook laksa in a Malay village, climbed a mountain with your kids in Morocco, or explored the shores of Lake Malawi by dugout canoe?

According to a new report called *The Spirit Of Adventure* by consumer trends think-tank the Future Laboratory, it's the latter. We are growing bored of simply lounging on the beach, and are looking for more meaningful experiences from our holidays. We want escapism but we don't want to switch off.

We are growing bored of simply lounging on the beach, and are looking for more meaningful experiences

The survey of 1,000 British travellers, tour operators and travel media found that 'Brits abroad' are not a homogeneous group. Among the types identified by the Future Laboratory are 'flashpackers' who refuse to slum it just because they like walking in the wilderness; 'slackpackers', who use websites like globalfreeloaders.com to secure free accommodation; and 'family adventurists' who think nothing of schlepping up mountains together and bedding down in remote lodges.

Martin Raymond, one of the authors of the report, says, 'What struck me was the shift away from passive to active holidays; the move towards greater risk as people seek engagement with cultures, environment and locale. People don't want to opt out any more – they want to mix and get involved.'

The really interesting part, he says, is that it's not age specific. 'The over-60s are throwing themselves into the fulfilment of volunteer breaks . . . with the same enthusiasm as gap-year students, as are thirtysomethings disillusioned with the rat race.'

So how did we become so bold? According to Raymond the research ties in with general trends. Consumers are 'insisting on authenticity and genuineness from brands and experiences. They want individually tailored services.'

And, as in other sectors, businesses are eager to cater for the new adventure-seeking holidaymaker. Established adventure operators such as Explore Worldwide, The Adventure Company and, as of this week (7 February 2005), Exodus, have created itineraries for families, from forest walks and horse-riding in Cuba to travelling across the Namib desert by truck.

Such is the popularity of this type of travel, The Adventure Company is diversifying further with the launch of dedicated trips for families with teens or infants, and single parents. Others are moving into the luxury adventure market with packages that combine hiking and other activities with stylish characterful accommodation. Both Explore and Guerba have introduced upmarket versions of their trips so that holidaymakers can retreat to the comfort of an air-conditioned heritage hotel after spending the day roughing it.

Books and websites are changing, too. Footprint has just launched a guide to Patagonia aimed at the 'flashpackers'. Similar guides to Belize, Guatemala and Southern Mexico are planned. A third of the holidays on takethefamily.com, launched last June, fall into the 'adventure' category.

Even backpackers, traditionally thought to be a breed apart, are part of the trend. In the past, if they didn't stand out for their ethnic gear, they certainly did for their penny-pinching and desire to get wasted. Now they, too, want to get off the well-worn path and are interested in social, cultural and environmental issues. According to Lonely Planet's travel information manager, Tom Hall: 'The backpacker is dead – Bondi beach is no longer filled with boozed-up budget travellers.'

Lonely Planet's own survey of almost 20,000 travellers, 15,000 of whom were aged 18-34, indicates that the new backpackers – or 'global nomads' – are degree educated, have strong opinions about social justice and world peace, and see travel as a culturally valuable stage on life's way. The report claims that 80% are single, of those 72% are women, and that half of all travellers say they are 'mid range' in terms of budget.

They take their favourite gadgets with them and are style conscious, too – they aren't about to start wearing tie-dyed T-shirts and ethnic jewellery just because they're in a foreign country. 'There's a new, savvy – even sexy – independent traveller who goes round the world armed with an iPod, photo mobile and state-of-the-art digital camera. She wears Diesel and Boxfresh, not Thai fisherman's pants,' says Hall.

Lonely Planet's survey suggests the hottest destinations for global nomads and flashpackers include Cuba, Sri Lanka and Cambodia, with Australia, Chile and Brazil high on the list of where young travellers plan to go next.

But they may just find they are not alone. The under-26s do not have a monopoly on adventure. Families, retired couples, 40-something career gappers and soul-searching singles are all taking a piece of the action, too.

Essential kit for global nomads

What's an iPod without accessories?
Battery running out and you're deep in the Cambodian jungle? Just launched TuneJuice gives eight hours more power. $19.95 (£10) from Griffin Technology at their website www.griffintechnology.com).

Road music
The iTrip attaches to the top of an iPod and broadcasts an FM signal so you can play your tunes through the radio (though it is illegal to use in the UK). Will make that camper-van journey across New Zealand even more memorable. $35 (£17.50) from Griffin Technology at their website www.griffintechnology.com.

Snorkelling soundtrack
Can't bear to be without music for a single second? Then take your iPod with you into the pool or sea. H2O Audio's waterproof casing comes complete with waterproof earphones, functional to a depth of 10 feet. Available from March 2005. $149.95, www.h2oaudio.com.

Old-school style
Forget Velcro sandals. Today's style-conscious nomads go for vintage-look Converse All Stars. From £29.99, www.converse.com.

The new backpackers – or 'global nomads' – are degree educated, have strong opinions about social justice and world peace, and see travel as a culturally valuable stage on life's way

---

Smart backpack
Planning to combine schlepping through the jungle with some serious city living? Then you need dual-purpose luggage. The straps of Mandarina Duck's smart rucksack tuck away to reveal a wheelie suitcase. £105-£125, Mandarina Duck, 16 Conduit Street, London W1S 2XL, and department stores (including Selfridges, Liberty, Harvey Nichols), www.mandarinaduck.com.

Protect your gear
Today's nomads are turning to high-tensile stainless steel security mesh to protect their kit. £44.99 from Blacks (0800 056 0127, or visit www.blacks.co.uk).

Passport to fun

Information for younger travellers

Travelling abroad is exhilarating, enjoyable, enriching and exciting, allowing you to let your hair down, relax and escape from it all. Through travel you'll discover new places, meet new people and experience different cultures. You'll remember your holidays for a very long time and that's why, whether it's a long weekend away with the girls, a week's sun, sea, sand and sangria with the boys or a trip of a lifetime around the world, you'll want to ensure that your holiday is remembered for all the right reasons.

With this in mind, the Foreign and Commonwealth Office has produced this guide featuring handy hints and travel tips so that you can enjoy yourself, confident that you're well prepared.

Be sure you're insured

You never know what's around the corner, especially when travelling abroad. Whether you're an adrenalin junkie or going away to enjoy some rest and relaxation, you need to make sure that you're covered for the type of holiday or activity you're planning.

Some typical costs for those without adequate insurance:
- Treatment of broken leg (in Europe) £5-6,000. OUCH!
- Treatment of broken leg (in USA) £10,000. That's gotta hurt.

Handy tips when shopping around for your insurance policy:
- Make sure comprehensive medical and repatriation cover is included.
- Make sure your whole trip is covered.
- Ensure all activities, especially hazardous sports, are covered.
- Disclose pre-existing medical conditions, including those of anyone you are travelling with. If you don't, it could affect your claim.
- If you have any doubts about your cover – check with your insurer before you go.

Make sure you 'know before you go'

Being able to reel off your 'Hola', 'Ciao' and 'Salut' greetings with confidence and panache while knowing your Greek 'Efharisto' from your Thai 'Korp kum kha' can make a huge difference to your trip and the reception you get when you're away.

Learning some of the local customs could also prevent you from inadvertently causing offence.

The best advice is:
- Plan ahead to avoid trouble – check out the latest FCO travel advice available online on their website at www.fco.gov.uk/knowbeforeyougo or by calling 020 7008 0232 / 0233.
- Get a good guidebook and read up on your destination. Make sure you know about local laws and customs, especially those relating to alcohol and drugs.
- Take a phrase book – you may enjoy learning a few words – it can be invaluable in case of emergencies.
- Respect local customs and dress codes. Think about what you wear and how you fit in. Ask your tour rep or local guide if you are unsure.
- Photographs – it's worth asking before you snap so as not to cause offence.

Passport to entry – check your visas!

For a smooth journey, check whether you have the right visas / documentation for all the countries you plan to visit before you go. In some countries, if you don't have the right paperwork, you won't be let in!
- Check visa requirements with your travel agent or the relevant Embassy/High Commission.
- Apply for your passport in good time. In the UK, advice on how to obtain a passport is available online at www.passport.gov.uk or by calling 0870 521 0410.
- Outside the UK, you should seek advice from the nearest British Consulate. Our consular staff can issue emergency passports and in some places full passports.
- It's worth checking the expiry date on your passport before you travel. If you turn up at check-in with an out-of-date passport you won't be allowed to travel. Make sure your passport is valid for a minimum of six months at the date of your return.

Drugs – be aware

Be aware of the consequences of becoming involved with drugs overseas. Obey the local laws. Using or transporting drugs abroad carries heavy penalties. In many countries you could be imprisoned for many years – often in grim conditions; fined; or deported for offences that may incur a lesser charge in the UK. You can even receive the death penalty in some countries. We cannot get you out of jail.

More than half the British people in jail overseas have been imprisoned for drug offences.
- Never carry packages through Customs for other people and do not sit in anyone else's vehicle when going through Customs or crossing a border.
- Many countries refuse to grant bail before trial and often detain people in solitary confinement.
- You will get a criminal record in the UK if caught with drugs abroad, prosecuted and found guilty.

- If you've been caught with drugs abroad, you're unlikely ever to be allowed to visit the country again.
- If you get injured or ill as a result of drugs, your holiday insurance may be invalidated and your tour operator can refuse to fly you home.

The healthy way to go

Being ill on holiday can be a misery – from painful sunburn to the infamous dodgy tummy – and with no home comforts or familiar remedies, it really can make or break a trip.

A few handy tips include:
- Make sure you visit your GP at least six weeks prior to going abroad to check that you are totally up to date with any vaccinations you might need and for advice on any additional health precautions.
- Check out the advice available online on the DOH website at www.doh.gov.uk/traveladvice and ask your travel agent about the medical facilities in the country you are visiting.
- Check that your medication is legal in the country you are travelling to and pack it in your hand luggage. If taking medication with you, also take the prescription and a GP's letter.
- If travelling within the EEA (European Economic Area) get an E111 from the Post Office or from the Department of Health by calling 0800 555 777 for free or reduced cost emergency medical treatment.
- For longer trips make sure you are up to date with dental and optical check-ups. Go to the dentist before you go and take a spare pair of glasses or your prescription – just in case!
- Be safe in the sun. Avoid excessive sunbathing, especially between 11am and 3pm, and wear a high factor sunscreen. If you're tired during the day, following a late night, take care not to fall asleep in the sun. Burning can increase the risk of skin cancer.
- Drink plenty of water. If you drink alcohol or use some kinds of drugs your body can become dehydrated, especially in a hot climate.

- Always use a condom. Ensure you pack a supply before you go as they are not always as readily available abroad and quality can differ depending on where you are.
- Find out the local emergency number and the address of the nearest hospital when you arrive overseas. Your holiday rep / local guide or hotel / guesthouse will know.

This information could help save a life.

Party party party!

Drunken tales can make great holiday stories and we all go away on holiday to have a good time – but fun shouldn't come at a price! Try to know your limits and make sure that you are taking care of yourself:
- Be aware that accidents are more likely to happen after using alcohol / taking drugs.

Make sure you visit your GP at least six weeks prior to going abroad to check that you are totally up to date with any vaccinations you might need

---

- Self-inflicted accidents come at a cost: If you have an accident or injure yourself while on drugs, or under the influence of alcohol, it is unlikely that your travel insurance will cover you. You may have to spend time in a foreign hospital, where they may not speak your language or you may need to be repatriated home at a huge cost.
- Make sure you're fit to fly. There are severe penalties for being drunk and disorderly onboard aircraft.
- Never drive after drinking or taking drugs or get in a car with someone who has. Try to share a cab with a friend. Never accept a lift from an unlicensed taxi, a stranger or someone you do not completely trust.

Make sure you remain vigilant however much fun you're having, and keep an eye out for your friends.

- If you are going to drink alcohol, know your limit. Remember that drinks served in bars overseas are often stronger than those in the UK.
- Consider very carefully whether you should leave the pub, club or party with someone you have just met. Be aware that the use of alcohol and drugs can lead to you being less alert, less in control and less aware of your environment.
- Be aware that drugs are sometimes used in rape. Once added to a drink they cannot normally be detected. Try to keep your drink with you at all times.
- Remain aware of other holidaymakers and acquaintances you have made. Rape and incidents of sexual assault are frequently perpetrated by 'acquaintances', however casual that acquaintance may be.

If you need us – what we can and cannot do

If you do get into trouble you can contact British Consular Staff around the world who may be able to help. It's worth checking you have the address and telephone number of the local British Embassy, High Commission or Consulate before you travel. Your rep/local guide, hotel/guesthouse or local police are likely to have this information.

In countries outside the European Union (EU) where we do not have any British Consular Officers, and where there is an embassy or consulate of another EU member state, you may be able to get help from the consular staff of that member state.

Can:
- Issue emergency passports, and, in some places, full passports.
- Contact relatives and friends and ask them to help you with money or tickets.
- Tell you how to transfer money.
- In an emergency, cash you a sterling cheque worth up to £100 into local currency, if supported by a valid banker's card.
- Help you get in touch with local lawyers, interpreters and doctors.
- Arrange for next of kin to be told of an accident or a death and advise on procedures.

- Visit you if you have been arrested or put in prison, and arrange for messages to be sent to relatives and friends.
- Put you in touch with organisations who help trace missing persons.
- Speak to the local authorities on your behalf.
- Only as a last resort, in exceptional circumstances, and as long as you meet certain strict rules, give you a loan to get you back to the UK, but only if there is no one else who can help you.

Cannot:
- Get you out of prison.
- Give legal advice or start court proceedings for you.
- Get you better treatment in hospital or prison than is given to local nationals.
- Investigate a crime.
- Pay your hotel, legal, medical or any other bills.
- Pay your travel costs, except in special circumstances.
- Do work normally done by travel agents, airlines, banks or motoring organisations.
- Get you somewhere to live, a job or work permit.
- Demand you be treated as British if you are a dual national in the country of your second nationality.

Top ten tips

- **Get insurance**. It can happen to you, so take out insurance. Make sure it's comprehensive and covers you for medical and repatriation costs as well as any dangerous sports or activities.
- **Have local knowledge**. Read up on local laws and customs to avoid offending people or breaking local laws, however unwittingly. Check out the FCO travel advice on their website: www.fco.gov.uk/knowbeforeyougo, or on 020 7008 0232/0233.
- **Be health aware**. Check out what jabs and health care you need with your GP at least six weeks before you set off. Remember to stock up on condoms or birth control and don't take any risks with unprotected sex, no matter how appealing it might seem at the time.

- **Avoid drugs**. When it comes to drugs, be aware of the consequences. Using drugs abroad carries heavy penalties, including death, and being a British citizen won't get you out of jail.
- **Be careful with alcohol**. If you are going to drink alcohol, know your limit. Accidents are more likely after using alcohol or drugs and as well as the pain and embarrassment, you're unlikely to be covered by your insurance.
- **Be vigilant**. Stay aware of what is going on around you and keep away from situations with which you do not feel comfortable. Be aware that drugs are sometimes used in rape and once added to a drink they cannot normally be detected, so try to keep your drink with you at all times.
- **Check visas**. Ensure you have the correct visas. If you plan to work outside of the EU, obtain a valid work permit before you go.
- **Take care of your belongings**. Keep an eye on your belongings and lock valuables away. Be careful when you're out and about – the beach and crowded streets are favourite places for pickpockets to operate. Make copies of your tickets, passport, insurance policy (plus 24-hour emergency number), itinerary and contact details and leave one at home – just in case.
- **Take enough money**. The FCO can't send you home for free if you run out, so ensure you have a return ticket, or enough funds to buy one.

- **Keep in touch**. Consider taking a roam-enabled mobile phone with you and use e-mail to keep in touch. Leave details of your travel itinerary with your family and friends; tell them of any change of plan.

Money (and spending it!)

Spending money abroad is easier than ever before! The following tips should help you when buying that new bikini for the beach or foreign footie shirt:

- Check the validity, expiry dates and cash available on your credit or debit card(s) ahead of you trip. It's best to know your spending capacities before they run out!
- Make sure you have back-up funds such as travellers' cheques, sterling, Euros or US dollars or a credit card you don't intend to use except in emergencies.
- Have a return ticket, or enough money to buy one.
- Always have some change in the local currency when you arrive in case you need to make a short telephone call, catch a taxi or get something to eat or drink.
- Check with your bank prior to going abroad whether you can use your debit/credit card in the country you are visiting.

- The above information is reprinted with kind permission from the Foreign and Commonwealth Office: for more information please visit their website at www.fco.gov.uk

© *Crown Copyright*

Risky business

Irresponsible parents put homes at risk as kids backpack without insurance

Of the 250,000 18- to 24-year-old backpackers leaving the UK over the next six months, one in three will travel without insurance. With their most popular activities being adventure sports, moped riding and drinking, backpackers are more likely to suffer accident and injury than holiday-makers. Considering that air ambulances alone cost more than £15,000, it is very easy to rack up a medical bill of over £100,000. Without travel insurance, families would have to find money to fund this privately, meaning that over 75,000 family homes will potentially be put at risk this year.

Says Tom Griffiths, Founder of gapyear.com, the UK's largest backpacker information site: 'We find it incredible that parents will not let their children drive a car without insurance, but will let them travel the world uninsured. This irresponsible behaviour is not only putting their children's lives at risk, but also their family homes, businesses and assets.'

With the busiest departure months fast approaching; backpackers beginning to swarm towards Sydney for Christmas and about to take advantage of the cheap fares in the New Year; it is vital that parents wake up to their responsibilities now.

Griffiths continues: 'Time and again we see backpackers and their parents disregarding the importance of insurance. Our research has shown that backpackers spend more time buying a penknife for their trip, than they do on insurance. For less than £1 per day, less than will be spent on beer, they will cover themselves. The busiest backpacking planning period is now. Our message to parents is: "Have you had the insurance discussion with your child yet? If not, why not?" It only took us 15 minutes to find five different quotes, less time than it takes to get into town to buy a guide book or one of the many less-than-vital travel gadgets.'

It is very easy to rack up a medical bill of over £100,000

Griffiths concludes: 'Insurance is boring and perceived as complicated and expensive, which is why many backpackers choose not to take it. I am one of those who backpacked in my early days without insurance. In hindsight I can't believe that I risked the family home and finances. It is terrifying to think that someone planning their trip right now may return home to a bankrupt family. Ignorant youngsters are one thing. Irresponsible parents are another. This is not scaremongering. This really could happen.'

Paul Dittmer from Columbus Direct who run specialist backpacker insurance NoWorriesInsurance.com, says: 'Most backpackers and their parents are unaware of the costs involved and how easy it is to get into financial trouble. Many think that if they aren't going to bungy jump or get involved in adventure sports, then they are unlikely to have accidents. In reality most accidents are the more common ones that we see back home, like slipping and breaking something, walking into things and traffic accidents.'

The cost of accidents

- **£150,000+** A backpacker who broke his neck diving into shallow water on Bondi Beach on Christmas Day.
- **£50,000** A backpacker felt ill on a mountain in Nepal. Her air ambulance bill and medical fees came to over £50,000.
- **£9,000** Cost of a broken thigh for a lad who fell off a donkey in Spain.
- **£3,000+** A broken ankle in Europe simply from falling off a kerb.

Most common backpacker accidents

1. Falling off mopeds
2. Falling over when drunk (out of bars, into roads etc.)
3. Diving into shallow water on a beach or in a pool.

Unfortunately many think that they are covered, but find out that they aren't.

3 common backpacker examples include:

1. Most insurance policies won't cover mopeds over 50 cc (many backpackers hire bigger bikes)

2. Most diving policies only cover you down to 30m (many divers dive deeper, which is often where the problems occur)

3. Sports and adventure sports you think are covered, not being covered e.g. kite-surfing, jet skiing, para-sailing often aren't.

3 top tips for buying insurance

1. Shop around. Be wary of new companies with little history and extremely cheap policies – they are cheap for a reason. Look for quality, which often may not be the cheapest

2. Write a list of EVERYTHING you might possibly do on your trip (e.g. you can ski in New Zealand) and get covered for all eventualities (adding sports on once travelling can be more expensive)

3. 'Unlimited medical costs' are more of a marketing gimmick than fact. The largest ever

Of the 250,000 18- to 24-year-old backpackers leaving the UK over the next six months, one in three will travel without insurance

medical bill was for around £900,000. Although the Government recommends a minimum of £5 million, £1-£3 million should be plenty for backpackers who are less likely to be travelling with children, suffer heart attacks etc.

How easy is it to shop around?
Staff at gapyear.com rang around/ went online to find a number of reputable quotes on Wednesday 13th October 2004. We asked for cover for a backing trip to Australia for six months to include bungy jumping

and white water rafting. The search took 15 minutes and we found five good quality quotes that ranged from £70 to £190.

We were surprised that we were unable to get cover from the following brands:

■ Youthtravel.com. Reason: do not cover bungy jumps
■ Tesco Insurance. Reason: do not cover backpackers.

This highlights the growing trend for parents to buy insurance from brands they trust or look right, but who may not have the right level of cover – which leaves their children 'un' or under-insured on their travels. All backpackers and their parents need to know exactly what they are being covered for. The brand selling the insurance is almost irrelevant.

■ The above information is re-printed courtesy of gapyear.com – visit www.gapyear.com for more.
© gapyear.com

Australia – still top dream holiday spot for Brits

Australia is still the number-one destination UK package holidaymakers would most like to visit, the 2004 Holiday Survey by MORI for ABTA has found

Australia is still the number-one destination UK package holidaymakers would most like to visit, the 2004 Holiday Survey by MORI for ABTA has found. But this year, when people were asked where they would go if money were no object, more people than ever said that they would choose a round-the-world trip.

Commenting on the findings, ABTA Chief Executive Ian Reynolds said: 'Australia has been the most dreamed-of destination for a number of years, but with cheaper airfares, it has become more accessible, and so many are able to make their dream of going to Australia come true. If this is the case, then it would also follow, that dreams are now more adventurous. There has been a significant rise in the number of round-the-world

tickets sold this year, and with more people from all ages with more disposable income, but with no time, they are daring to dream of a round-the-world trip.'

Notes
Between 9 October and 5 November 2004, MORI surveyed 724 people, across the UK, who had taken a

package holiday in the previous 12 months.
Frances Tuke

■ The above information is reproduced with kind permission from the Association of British Travel Agents – visit www.abta.com, or see page 41 for address details.
© ABTA 2004

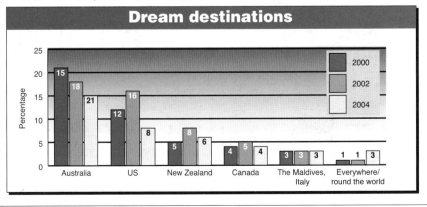

Travel agents and Internet bookings

The Internet is now firmly established as a booking tool for holidays, with 19% of holidaymakers booking their package holiday online – six times the number compared to the year 2000, the 2004 Holiday Survey by MORI for ABTA has found

The Internet is now firmly established as a booking tool for holidays, with 19% of holidaymakers booking their package holiday online – six times the number compared to the year 2000, the 2004 Holiday Survey by MORI for ABTA has found. Yet 72% of these package holidaymakers said that they would be considering booking holidays in the next two years through a high street travel agent.

Price is a major determining factor for why people use the web and 70% of those who have used the Internet for holiday bookings, said that they would be prepared to return to travel agents if they provided better deals. But most high street travel agents are proving that they are giving customers what they want. Consumer trust in travel agents has

> *70% of those who have used the Internet for holiday bookings, said that they would be prepared to return to travel agents if they provided better deals*

improved by a third this year compared to two years ago – while 95% of those who had used a travel agent said that they have received a very good or fairly good service.

Seventy-five per cent of package holidaymakers said that they used travel agents for a source of information – compared to 57% who used the web for information – but 71% of

holidaymakers with broadband access said that they were inclined to browse travel sites more often.

Interestingly another survey this year done by the Co-op Travel Trading Group found that booking via the Internet was slower. An agent will take on average 15 minutes to find a best holiday price compared to an average 111 minutes taken by consumers trawling the web.

'ABTA members have always been at the forefront of providing information and selling travel on the net, and recently they have invested a lot of money in making their sites more user-friendly and efficient,' said ABTA chief executive Ian Reynolds. 'Although consumers are preoccupied by price, our high street travel agent members have diversified, and those that have invested in high quality service and expertise are succeeding in selling high value holidays of all description.'
Frances Tuke

■ The above information is reproduced with kind permission from the Association of British Travel Agents – for more information visit at www.abta.com or see page 41 for address details.

© ABTA 2004

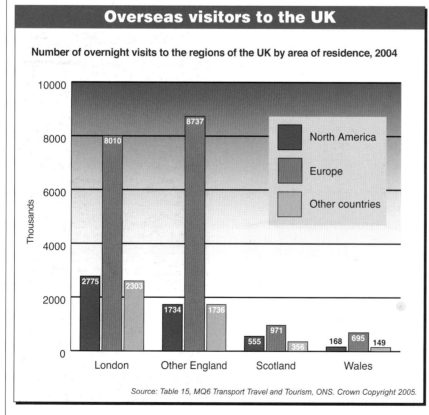

Overseas visitors to the UK

Number of overnight visits to the regions of the UK by area of residence, 2004

Legend:
- North America
- Europe
- Other countries

London: 2775, 8010, 2303
Other England: 1734, 8737, 1736
Scotland: 555, 971, 356
Wales: 168, 695, 149

Y-axis: Thousands (0, 2000, 4000, 6000, 8000, 10000)

Source: Table 15, MQ6 Transport Travel and Tourism, ONS. Crown Copyright 2005.

Branson promises to send tourists into space by 2007

By David Derbyshire, Science Correspondent

Seasoned Sir Richard Branson watchers could be forgiven for thinking there was nothing left on the planet to escape the red and white Virgin logo.

But yesterday (27 Sept 2004), the entrepreneur revealed that his ambitions were no longer restricted to the Earth and announced that Virgin would be sending the first tourists into space within three years.

In a £14 million deal, Virgin Galactic is licensing five 'space liners', built by the American team responsible for the world's first private space flight.

Prices for the three-hour flight – during which tourists will spend three to four minutes weightless and see the curvature of the Earth – are expected to start at £100,000.

Sir Richard yesterday predicted that 3,000 amateur astronauts could be flying in space over a five-year period.

Although the announcement appeared to have all the hallmarks of a Branson publicity stunt, the credentials of his partners are impressive.

The deal was signed with Mojave Aerospace Ventures (MAV), a company set up by the aviation pioneer Burt Rutan and the co-founder of Microsoft, Paul Allen, to exploit the technology developed for the craft SpaceShipOne.

In June, MAV's SpaceShipOne reached 62 miles, becoming the first privately funded craft to leave the atmosphere.

Sir Richard – whose business empire has included music publishing, record stores, cola, condoms, airlines, vodka and personal finance – told the *Telegraph* that he would be one of the first passengers on board the five-seater space planes.

'Every child dreams of going into space,' he said. 'I'm in a position to make that a reality. There are thousands of people who can afford a reasonable price to get the ball rolling. Hopefully we can bring the pricing down to a level where millions can afford it.'

Virgin is hoping to use a larger version of SpaceShipOne. The first craft will be called VSS Enterprise – after the Star Trek spaceship.

Unlike traditional rockets, Enterprise will be carried to 47,000ft slung beneath a conventional plane where its rocket engines will be ignited, sending it upwards at three times the speed of sound.

Sir Richard predicted that 3,000 amateur astronauts could be flying in space over a five-year period

As the craft reaches the top of the atmosphere, passengers will experience a few minutes of weightlessness.

The craft will then adjust its wings into a 'high drag' configuration so its speed is controlled as it descends and glides back to the Earth.

It is unlikely that travellers will be able to get insurance. They will probably be asked to sign waivers absolving Virgin of any responsibility should things go wrong.

But Sir Richard said: 'It's far safer than Nasa's space rockets in that we don't have to blast our way out of the earth's atmosphere with all the inherent risks of incredible temperatures.

'I expect to go up and my children would love to come up too. I don't feel uncomfortable about that.'

The first space tourist was Dennis Tito, an American businessman who paid around £11 million for a trip on a Soyuz rocket to the International Space Station in April 2001.

The second was Mark Shuttleworth, a South African businessman, who visited the space station the following year.

Sir Richard said: 'Because space travel has been run by the Government and not by entrepreneurial individuals, it hasn't really moved forward.

'Billions of dollars have been wasted in grandiose projects that have not achieved a lot. Now private enterprise is getting interested and I think that in my lifetime we may be able to go to the next phase of hotels in space and possibly going to the moon.'

He added: 'We've already had plenty of calls from people who have heard about this. Most people would love to go to space.'

David Learmount, the operations and safety editor of *Flight International* magazine, said: 'This is just the kind of thing Branson absolutely loves, because it gets him maximum publicity. But the technology is there and well tested – it's plausible.'

The good tourist guide

In this extract from *The Rough Guide to a Better World*, travel writer Richard Hammond provides a practical exploration of what it means to travel responsibly

Top tips for responsible travel

Tourism has become a major world industry. We are travelling further and in far greater numbers than ever before. We journey into the heart of rainforests and up the highest mountains, soak up the sun on tropical beaches and dive in coral reefs. We gaze in wonder at the mighty ruins of ancient civilisations and get up close and personal with the most amazing wildlife on earth.

The cost of flying has reduced dramatically in a decade, which means we can choose long-haul trips that were previously unaffordable. Mexico, Malaysia and Thailand are no longer just the domain of intrepid backpackers or the leisurely wealthy, while charter flights are now common to developing countries like Brazil, Sri Lanka, and The Gambia.

Tourism – and associated activities – generates over 10 per cent of Global Domestic Product and employs 200 million people

According to the World Travel and Tourism Council, tourism – and associated activities – generates over 10 per cent of Global Domestic Product and employs 200 million people. There are nearly 700 million international travellers a year, a figure set to double by 2020.

But while this staggering growth of tourism has expanded our holiday options and boosted revenue, investment and jobs, it has also become a focus for concern – particularly in relation to developing countries. The economic prosperity that tourism brings to these destinations can be cancelled out by its impact on the environment and local communities. Fragile coastal ecosystems are creaking under the strain of mass hotel complexes, local water supplies are drying up through over-demand, and ancestral homes are vanishing to make way for tourism development.

All of this means that the type of holiday we choose and what we do while on holiday is becoming important, not just for safeguarding our own enjoyment but for the future prosperity of the destinations themselves – the very places we so love to visit.

Developing countries in particular are capturing an increasing share of the global tourism market. Fourteen of the top 20 long-haul destinations are now in developing countries.

For many destinations visitor numbers have doubled, or even tripled, in a decade. This trend provides an engine of economic development for poorer countries.

Tourism has become the main money earner for a third of developing nations, and the primary source of foreign exchange earnings for most of the 49 least developed countries. And as tourism is based around natural and cultural resources – something even many of the poorest countries have in abundance – it can provide opportunities where few other industries are available.

What's more, the infrastructure associated with tourism development (roads, electricity, communications, piped water) can provide essential services for rural communities. The money tourism brings can also help local wildlife and environmental conservation – many of the world's protected natural areas are subsidised by tourism income and would struggle to survive without it. But alongside the economic benefits, tourism can add to the difficulties faced by people in the developing world.

The very asset that tourism depends on – the cultural and natural heritage – is also the daily resource of millions of local people, and can be threatened by exploitation and

abuse. The drive for tourism development can lead to displacement of local and indigenous peoples, cultural degradation, and the distortion of local economies and social structures. Local people can also be socially and economically marginalised by tourism, especially in the all-inclusive package holiday market. When tourism multinationals own every element of the chain – from travel agent to tour operator, airline, hotel, and even local ground transportation companies – local people are deprived of a fair share in the profits of tourism; indeed, many earn nothing at all.

The mantra of the 1990s eco-traveller, 'Take only photographs, leave only footprints', was born from the realisation that tourism could provide positive benefits to conservation and the environment. The International Ecotourism Society defines ecotourism as: 'Responsible travel to natural areas that conserves the environment and promotes the wellbeing of local people.' This has now developed into a deeper understanding that the places we visit are other people's homes. The beaches we lie on are their back yards; the bars we drink in are their locals; the vegetable markets are their sources of food; and the national parks are there to protect their land.

'Responsible travel' is becoming a more common feature in popular holiday brochures – with the focus on encouraging the beneficial side of tourism while providing for environmental protection and remembering responsibilities to local people and cultures. It's about having a fantastic holiday that minimises the harm to the environment and doesn't contribute to the exploitation of local people. 'Community tourism' is

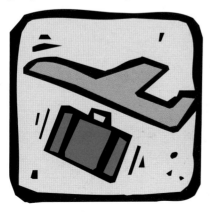

another term used by the travel industry, referring to responsible holidays that aren't necessarily nature-based (as in ecotourism), but where the emphasis is on the fact that local people run or organise the holidays.

A single passenger on a return London to New York flight produces more carbon dioxide than the average UK motorist does in a year

---

Given that many of us are increasingly aware of social, cultural and environmental issues in travel, when it comes to actually booking our holidays, how can we put our money where our mouths are? Choosing a responsible holiday tour operator is a good place to start. Some travel companies now include a responsible travel policy that offers a better exchange of culture with local people as well as ensuring some of the money you're paying goes towards the local communities. The Association of Independent Tour Operators (AITO), which represents about 150 independently owned UK tour operators, provides its own Responsible Tourism Guidelines that are now part of its membership criteria. Its website lists operators that have been given two or three stars for their performance in responsible tourism. Increasingly, operators are incorporating a written responsible travel policy. This should describe how their trips benefit conservation and local people. Some operators give a donation to a local charity or help fund local conservation and community projects in the destination.

Another place to research ethical holidays is *The Good Alternative Travel Guide* produced by Tourism Concern, a charity that campaigns for fair trade in tourism. This Guide lists holidays in some of the world's most beautiful regions, from walking the songlines of central Australia with Aboriginal guides to visiting the Inuit above the Arctic Circle.

Unsurprisingly, the net is a great resource to find out about tours organised by local people. For example, ResponsibleTravel.com is an online agent offering holidays to 140 countries – from B&Bs in Snowdonia to swimming with humpback whales in Tonga. TourismConcern.org.uk also offers a wealth of resources.

Air travel has become a major contributor to global warming – even if we book a holiday through a responsible operator, if it involves flying great distances it can hardly be said to be doing the environment much good. A single passenger on a return London to New York flight produces more carbon dioxide than the average UK motorist does in a year.

When we do have to travel by air, organisations such as Future Forests or Climate Care accept donations to support the development of renewable and clean energy projects that reduce carbon dioxide emissions. Both organisations provide travellers with tools on their websites online at www.futureforests.com and www.co2.org to work out what should be paid to offset the share of the pollution generated from a flight. It's also worth considering booking flights through North South Travel whose profits are all donated to grassroots development organisations, mostly in Africa. Many organisations point responsible travellers in the right direction – the Foreign and Commonwealth Office runs a 'Know Before You Go' campaign, which encourages holidaymakers to familiarise themselves with the customs and culture of holiday destinations. It also backs the Travel Foundation, a charity set up to help manage the travel industry more sustainably. A number of mainstream and niche tour operators offer the opportunity to make a donation to this charity when you book a holiday.

It is also possible to find travel and tourism companies that have been 'eco-certified'. There is no one global accreditation scheme for green or fair trade tourism, but several individual schemes recognise travel companies and projects that act more responsibly.

Green Globe Asia Pacific is a benchmarking, certification and improvement system for sustainable travel and tourism. The Ecotourism Certificate programme in Australia provides accreditation for ecological sustainability and natural area management.

The Fair Trade in Tourism South Africa trademark recognises certain special tourism ventures for their efforts in sustainable tourism. The Tourism for Tomorrow Awards are one of a range of awards for ethical or sustainable tourism that recognise projects which have made a positive contribution towards local natural and cultural environments, and improved the impact of tourism on the environment. AITO also has an annual award which is given to one of its members that has shown commitment to responsible tourism.

There are many things we can do on holiday which not only support local communities but also add to the enjoyment of a trip. For example,

by using local guides rather than expatriates, we can gain a better insight into the environment and culture – and boost local employment opportunities. We can further benefit local economies by buying food and souvenirs from local markets or craft cooperatives, not simply from hotel lobby shops, which are unlikely to pass much value back to the producers. Markets are also fantastic places to meet local people. It's often the people we meet that are the most memorable experience of a great holiday.

And once back in the UK, it's possible to buy crafts from developing countries through the Traidcraft mail-order catalogue or one of the British Association of Fair Trade shops, which ensure producers are paid reasonable wages and work in good conditions.

It's a mistake to assume that our holidays are insignificant compared to the enormity of the global travel and tourism industry. But a single

trip can make a difference to someone's life...the mountain guide, the village market trader, the local community group that receives a donation from a tour operator. Responsible travel and positive actions by travellers can reverse the impact of destructive tourism, can genuinely contribute towards good global development and can help preserve the beauty of the world for future generations.

■ This is an edited extract of *The Rough Guide to a Better World*, a Rough Guide publication supported by DFID, and was first published in the Department for International Development's 'Developments' magazine. The book was available free from all UK Post Offices from 29 November 2004. You can order a free copy online at the URL www.roughguide-betterworld.com, or visit the DFID's website at www.dfid.gov.uk to find out more.
© Richard Hammond

Are we loving our heritage to death?

Fake statues in Florence. A rope around Stonehenge. Is this the only way we'll get to see the world's great sights in the future? Oliver Bennett investigates

There seems to be an awful lot of interest in the world's cultural monuments. If it's not Dan Cruickshank's *Round The World In 80 Treasures*, then it's the BBC's *50 Things To Do Before You Die*, or the current search for the seven modern wonders of the world. At some point in our lives, we've all got to see Machu Picchu and the Pyramids, haven't we?

Well, an increasingly vocal group of conservationists, consultants and non-governmental agencies want tourists and tour operators alike to think more carefully; even to consider alternatives. Because tourist congestion can prove dangerous to the health of the world's must-see monuments, and working out how to manage the 'carrying capacity' of

sites (to use the jargon) is becoming an urgent priority.

Working out how to manage the 'carrying capacity' of sites (to use the jargon) is becoming an urgent priority

---

Machu Picchu, the Peruvian site where 2,500 visitors a day arrive in high season, is a case in point. John Hemming has seen tourism escalate since he first visited in 1960. 'It's the most important site in Latin America and if you're over there you have to go,' he says. But he believes it's right

that visitor numbers be restricted to combat erosion.

Wear and tear is even a concern for British day trippers. When Hadrian's Wall Path Trail opened last year, many rejoiced, but since then an unexpected 400,000 walkers have trodden the path and archaeologists are now concerned for its welfare.

Such is the paradox of modern tourism: that sites have to be protected and promoted at the same time. 'Some of the world's most important architectural landscapes have become victims of their own success,' says Colin Amery of the World Monuments Fund (WMF), which produces a Watch List of the 100 Most Endangered Sites every two years. 'Publicity is often used to attract funds for conservation work, but it can be a double-edged sword. From the Great Wall of China to the temples of Angkor in Cambodia, drastic compromises are being made to accommodate swelling visitor numbers.' A few, he argues, shouldn't be visited at all. 'As far as Easter Island and Shackleton's Hut in Antarctica are concerned, it is better these places exist unvisited than are destroyed by development to accommodate tourists.'

From the Great Wall of China to the temples of Angkor in Cambodia, drastic compromises are being made to accommodate swelling visitor numbers

---

There are now 611 cultural sites on the Unesco World Heritage List, 29 of which are considered at serious risk (see whc.unesco.org), and each listing potentially stimulates tourism. 'The level of tourism is much higher than it was 20 years ago and management issues should have been forecast,' says Susan Denyer of the International Council on Monuments and Sites (Icomos), a non-governmental body that advises Unesco. 'It's a major problem. Given cheaper air travel and greater mobility, people can now see these sites. One can't blame them for it.'

Dr Nicholas Stanley-Price, director-general of the International Centre for the Study of the Preservation and Restoration of Cultural Property (Iccrom), thinks the onus lies with site management rather than the tourists. 'We'd like to maximise people's ability to visit these places and to encourage local economies as well as help develop a sense of place. But we don't want to kill the goose that laid the golden egg.' Which is why the running of such places is critical.

There are several methods currently used to limit damage. Timed tickets are increasingly popular to reduce footfall. Then there's the growing practice of charging higher entrance fees to drive mass tourism out of the market: a method that, among others, the Taj Mahal and the tomb of Queen Nefertari in Egypt have adopted. 'The trouble with this approach is that some find it elitist,' says Dr Stanley-Price. Two-tier pricing policies can help with local access, as happens at the Taj Mahal and the desert city of Petra in Jordan.

Indeed, perhaps rich international tourists should always expect to pay more. After all, if you can go around the world to see a monument, then you can afford to pay an entrance fee.

'Sustainable tourism means making the richer countries of the world pay to help protect humanity's shared heritage,' says Amery. 'Hence, hotel and tourist taxes are essential to pay conservation and management bills, and the high-end should pay when

access is an issue.' In which case it's important to make sure the fees and taxes go to the right place.

Additionally, some monuments limit physical access, as English Heritage did when it roped off the stone circle at Stonehenge.

Another growing policy is to try to steer people away from the iconic sites: for instance, English Heritage now hopes to relieve pressure on Stonehenge by guiding visitors towards the area's wider neolithic landscape. This is difficult as tourists will always want to see the Big One, which is why conservationists are appealing to tourists, to make them understand that their gratification can contribute to a monument's degradation.

'We've got to get tourists to take on their responsibilities as well as rights,' says Denyer. 'One of the ways to do this is through guidebooks.' Icomos and Iccrom have been working with publishers, including Lonely Planet and the Tourist Club Of Italy, to try and raise awareness of the perils of congestion. Some may opt to under-publicise key sights.

To which some tourists might say: what possible harm am I doing? Well, a recent paper at the University Libre de Brussels suggested that even walking and body heat play a deleterious part. 'An individual walking slowly (3.2 km/h) in an environment of 15°C develops a heat power around 200W, freeing 100g of water vapour and 100g of CO_2,' it reported.

But there is a last resort that will assuage tourists and conservationists. 'I believe that one of the greatest hopes for monuments is the use of facsimiles,' says Simon Beeching, spokesman for the Travelwatch

Taj Mahal   Stonehenge   Machu Picchu

environmental consultancy. Fakes, in other words – which are already more widespread than many would imagine, including replica sculptures in Florence and on Mayan sites, and reproduction caves at Lascaux in France and Altimira in Spain.

'It's extraordinary how popular the replica cave art at Lascaux is,' says Dr Stanley-Price. 'Somehow, people don't feel they're being cheated. It's a totally acceptable solution and provided it's done well, there's no loss of atmosphere.'

It could yet be the best insurance against our loving the wonders of the world to death.

Machu Picchu
500,000 visitors a year
The Inca citadel has long grappled with problems of tourist congestion and access, and numbers are growing at 6% a year. Last year, a landslip occurred in the valley below and Unesco has threatened to put it on its endangered list. Visitors are already subject to restrictions. 'The Inca Trail [which leads to the citadel] is now closed to casual travellers,' says John Hemming. 'You have to go in a tour, which is not altogether bad.' A long-running saga has been the proposal of a cable car.

Angkor
1 million visitors
Cambodia's Angkor Archaeological Park – the 12th-century complex that includes Angkor Wat – is experiencing pressure from increasing visitor numbers. The World Monuments Fund and Cambodian authorities are examining ways to address visitor impact, particularly on Phnom Bakheng (famed for its sunset watching) and create a 'conservation management plan'. It has a two-tier pricing system: Cambodians go free; foreigners pay £12 for a day pass.

Forbidden City
7m visitors
Most of the visitors that cross the ancient stone floors of the Imperial City are Chinese, so the government is reluctant to limit access, but the WMF believes some kind of limits must soon be set or the city will risk irreversible damage. A restoration plan is now in place and due to be completed in 2020. The aim of the plan is to 'restore the solemnity, sublimity and glory of the Imperial Palace' and use timed tickets only.

Pompeii
2m visitors
The Roman town is one of the best known sites in the world – and also one of the most threatened. Visitor numbers have shot up from 863,000 in 1981 to around two million today. But many of the houses that were open in the 50s are now closed and Pompeii was included on the World Monuments Watch List of 100 Most Endangered Sites in 1996, 1998 and 2000. A 'conservation master plan' has ensued.

Taj Mahal
3m visitors
The Taj Mahal is the single most visited monument in India – in 2003 it lured three million people. All well and good, but it has been through various crises: pollution, fear of terrorism and congestion, which was barely dented when the admission fee for foreign visitors shot up in 2001 from 22p to £14. 'Unless you are the late Princess of Wales, you are never alone at the Taj Mahal,' says Colin Amery of the WMF. 'Timed tickets and strict rationing of numbers is beginning to make the Taj a more magical experience.' One plan proposes to close the Taj Mahal off altogether, so visitors could only view it from afar.

Sustainable tourism means making the richer countries of the world pay to help protect humanity's shared heritage

---

Acropolis
500,000 visitors
The Acropolis, a compulsory visit for all who visit Athens, hosts around half a million tourists a year, paying £12 each, and it is constantly being monitored for overcrowding. As with Stonehenge, visitors are encouraged to see it in the wider context, although the much-vaunted Acropolis Museum is still awaited.

Alhambra
2.2m visitors
The Alhambra was visited by 2.2m last year and the management decided to limit visitor numbers this season by offering timed visits. A total of 7,700 tourists a day will be allowed: 4,200 in the morning, 3,500 in the afternoon, thus avoiding 'crushes of up to 5,000 people'.

© *Guardian Newspapers Limited 2005*

...IT COULD BE THE TAJ MAHAL... OR IT COULD BE A PYRAMID...

An ecotourism glossary

Information from People and the Planet

Aboriginal: Refers to the original inhabitants of a country and their descendants. The term is used mainly in Australia and Canada. See also: First Nations, indigenous people.[1]

ABTA: Association of British Travel Agents. The trade association of large tour operators.

All-inclusive: A resort providing accommodation, food and all facilities (e.g. beach and watersports) internally, so that visitors have no need to leave the resort.[1]

ATOL: Air Travel Organisers' Licence. A bonding scheme run by the Civil Aviation Authority. If your tour operator is a member of ATOL, you are guaranteed a refund if the company goes into liquidation.

Backpacker: A (usually young) independent traveller; typically carries a rucksack and stays in cheap, locally owned accommodation.[1]

Community: A mutually supportive, geographically specific social unit such as a rural village or tribe. In an urban, Western context, the phrase is often used more loosely, to describe people with common interests, ethnic origins, etc.[1]

Community tourism: A shorter term for community-based tourism.[1]

Community-based tourism: Tourism that consults, involves and benefits a local community, especially in the context of rural villages in developing countries and indigenous peoples.[1]

Conservation (nature): Protection against irreversible destruction and other undesirable changes, including the management of human use of organisms or ecosystems to ensure such use is sustainable.

Customised itineraries: A holiday schedule drawn up by a tour operator specifically for one client or group, usually including flight, accommodation and transport. Sometimes called tailor-made holidays.[1]

Developed countries/nations/world: See the West.

People & the Planet

Developing countries/nations/world: The world's less wealthy nations, mostly former colonies: i.e. most of Asia, Africa, Latin America and the South Pacific. Also sometimes referred to as the South.[1]

Development: A process of economic and social transformation that defies simple definition. Though often viewed as a strictly economic process involving growth and diversification of a country's economy, development is a qualitative concept that entails complex social, cultural, and environmental changes. There are many models of what 'development' should look like and many different standards of what constitutes 'success'.

Domestic tourism: Holidays taken within the tourist's own country. The volume of domestic tourism is hard to quantify but has been estimated at three to five times greater than international tourism.[1]

Ecology: Originally defined by Ernst Haeckel in 1866, ecology is the study of the relationships that develop among living organisms and between these organisms and the environment.

Economic growth: The change over a period of time in the value (monetary and non-monetary) of goods and services and the ability and capacity to produce goods and services. It is economic growth which generates the wealth necessary to provide social services, health care, and education. It is the basis for ongoing job creation. However, sustainable development requires that there be a change in the nature of economic growth, to ensure that goods and services are produced by environmentally sound and economically sustainable processes. This will require efficient use of resources, value-added processing, sustained yield management of renewable resources, and the consideration and accounting of all externalities and side-effects involved in the extraction, processing, production, distribution, consumption, and disposal of those goods.

Economy: What human beings do. The activity of managing resources and producing, distributing, and consuming goods and services.

Ecotourism: According to the US-based Ecotourism Society, 'Ecotourism is responsible travel to natural areas that conserves the environment and sustains the well-being of local people.' In the UK, the phrase green travel is sometimes preferred.[1]

Endangered species: Species of plants or animals threatened with extinction because their numbers have declined to a critical level as a result of overharvesting or because their habitat has drastically changed. That critical level is the minimum viable population (MVP), and represents the smallest number of breeding pairs required to maintain the viability of species.

Environment: A combination of the various physical and biological elements that affect the life of an organism. Although it is common to refer to 'the' environment, there are in fact many environments e.g., aquatic or terrestrial, microscopic to

global, all capable of change in time and place, but all intimately linked and in combination constituting the whole earth/atmosphere system.

Environmentally-sound: The maintenance of a healthy environment and the protection of life-sustaining ecological processes. It is based on thorough knowledge and requires or will result in products, manufacturing processes, developments, etc. which are in harmony with essential ecological processes and human health.

Ethical tourism: See Responsible tourism.

Fair trade: Equitable, non-exploitative trade between developing world suppliers and Western consumers.[1]

First Nations: A collective term for the original, pre-European inhabitants of the US, Canada, Hawaii, Australia and New Zealand. In individual countries, different terms are sometimes used, for example, Aboriginal, indigenous, tribal, Indian, First Peoples, Native American, AmerIndian.[1]

Green travel: A UK alternative to the American term ecotourism.[1]

Independent traveller: Someone who travels without booking a package tour.[1]

Indigenous people: The original inhabitants of a country and their descendants. Indigenous communities are often, but not always, tribal peoples and the two terms are often and easily confused. See also First Nations, Aboriginal.[1]

Local communities / people: People living in tourist destinations, especially in the rural developing world.[1]

Multinational corporation: See Transnational corporation.

National conservation strategies: Plans that highlight country-level environmental priorities and opportunities for sustainable management of natural resources, following the example of the World Conservation Strategy published by the World Conservation Union (IUCN) in 1980. Though governments may support preparation for the strategies, they are not bound to follow IUCN's recommendations.

Native Americans: A collective term for the indigenous people of the Americas. Also First Nations, AmerIndians, American Indians, Indians.[1]

NGO: Non-governmental organisation: an independent pressure group or campaigning organisation, usually non-profit.[1]

North, the: See West, the.

Package tour: A holiday combining transport and accommodation in an inclusive price.[1]

Pro-poor tourism: Tourism that benefits poor people in developing-world tourist destinations.[1]

Proper resource pricing: The pricing of natural resources at levels which reflect their combined economic and environmental values.

Responsible tourism: Tourism that aims to avoid harmful impacts on people and environments. Sometimes referred to as ethical tourism. Other similar concepts include People First Tourism, reality tourism, etc.[1]

South, the: See Developing countries.

Sustainable development: Sustainable development has as many definitions as subscribers. In essence, it refers to economic development that meets the needs of all without leaving future generations with fewer natural resources than those we enjoy today. It is widely accepted that achieving sustainable development requires balance between three dimensions of complementary change:

- Economic (towards sustainable patterns of production and consumption)
- Ecological (towards maintenance and restoration of healthy ecosystems)
- Social (towards poverty eradication and sustainable livelihoods).

Sustainable tourism: Tourism that does not degrade the environment or local cultures/societies.[1]

Third World, the: Now generally referred to as either developing countries or the South.[1]

Tourists: Holiday-makers, mainly (but no longer exclusively) from the West. The term is sometimes used to distinguish package tourists from independent travellers, but can be used to mean anyone going on holiday.[1]

Transnational corporation: Correctly, a large company with shareholders in more than one country. The term is often used more loosely to mean any large, powerful, Western-owned company.[1]

Tribal peoples: People living in close-knit social units based on kinship ties and shared belief systems. While most remaining tribal communities are indigenous, not all indigenous peoples still live tribally. (On the other hand, for example, many 'hill-tribes' in northern Thailand migrated there fairly recently from southern China, making them tribal but not indigenous to Thailand.)[1]

West, the: The world's rich nations: i.e. Western Europe, the US, Canada, Australia, New Zealand and (economically, although perhaps not culturally) Japan.[1]

World Commission on Environment and Development: Established by the United Nations General

KEEP TO DESIGNAT PATH

Assembly in 1983 to examine international and global environmental problems and to propose strategies for sustainable development. Chaired by Norwegian Prime Minister Gro Harlem Brundtland, the independent commission held meetings and public hearings around the world and submitted a report on its inquiry to the General Assembly in 1987.

World Summit on Sustainable Development (WSSD): The World Summit on Sustainable Development took place from 26 August to 4 September 2002 in Johannesburg, South Africa. Governments, UN agencies, and civil society organisations came together to assess progress since the UN Conference on Environment and Development held in Rio in 1992 (hence the title 'Rio + 10' for the Johannesburg meeting). Sustainable development is defined in the report from the Rio meeting as being 'economic progress which meets all of our needs without leaving future generations with fewer resources than those we enjoy'.

World Tourism Organisation (WTO): A UN-affiliated organisation based in Madrid and comprising government and industry representatives, that compiles statistics and guidelines and promotes global tourism.[1]

World Travel and Tourism Council (WTTC): An organisation based in Brussels and London and made up of the chief executives of the world's largest travel companies, that lobbies on behalf of the tourism industry.[1]

Notes

1. Source: *The Community Tourism Guide* by Mark Mann, published by Earthscan Publications, London, 2001.

■ The above information is reprinted with kind permission from Planet 21, an independent charity providing a well-illustrated educational website on sixteen key themes linking people and the environment – for more information please visit www.peopleandplanet.net or see page 41 for their address details.

© Planet 21

An even greener and more pleasant land

Most people's idea of a responsible holiday is somewhere long-haul and exotic. But you could always take one very much closer to home . . .

The truth is, going on holiday is rarely environmentally sound. Just by flying out of the country your personal contribution to global warming goes way up. A return trip across the Atlantic is roughly equivalent to a year's motoring. Stay in the UK and you are already picking up the greenie points. But travelling responsibly is not simply a case of reducing pollution. Minimising environmental damage, supporting local economies and being sensitive to cultural differences is as relevant to a trip through the English countryside as a visit to a Costa Rican rainforest.

These concepts needn't be complex; it's simple to start travelling responsibly within the UK. With rural communities being depleted by urban migration, spending your money at locally owned businesses strengthens their economy and provides people with a reason to stay rather than leave. So shop locally for self-catering holidays, don't stock up at the supermarket and haul it all with you. In the same way that many wildlife parks in Africa need the support of tourists to survive, English nature reserves also depend on tourist expenditure. Traffic jams in the city are bad enough but gridlock in the countryside somehow seems even worse. Reduce pollution and congestion, take local transport once you get there, ride a bike or walk. English rural communities have strong cultural identities, different from yet no less valid than modern urban attitudes. Be respectful of these cultures. Talk to people in the pub. Buy them a beer rather than sniggering at their accents. You might be given local knowledge that can really improve your stay.

Travelling responsibly in England doesn't just mean changing your attitude, there is a growing array of responsible travel offerings to tap into. During the Foot and Mouth Crisis it came as a surprise for many to learn that this country had a vibrant rural tourism industry; rural tourism in England is estimated to be worth £14 billion per annum. With vast tracts of the countryside in virtual or actual quarantine the estimated damage to the domestic holiday market exceeded the economic impact to agriculture. The growth of responsible tourism practices in the UK has partly come about as a reaction to Foot and Mouth. Small tourism businesses have realised the advantage of supporting each other. They have also realised the obvious; that people come to see the countryside and it is in their economic interest to preserve that countryside. As a result, whether it's for a day out, a weekend break or an annual family fortnight, there are now many hotels, restaurants, activities and attractions across England with well-developed responsible tourism policies and practices. At one end of the scale you can relax responsibly at a rural boutique hotel that serves gourmet organic meals made from local produce. Or if you want more tangible proof that you are a responsible traveller you can get dirt under your fingernails on a working conservation holiday.

Several regions of England have developed integrated responsible tourism policies. They encourage local businesses to operate more responsibly, promote public transport geared towards tourist routes, implement recycling schemes and support conservation programmes. Cumbria Tourist Board and the Lake District National Park Authority are working on a scheme called 'Car Free, Care Free' to reduce traffic congestion in the Lake District. By co-operating with local transport companies they have provided bus services connecting boat trips on the lakes with towns and beauty spots. One of their partners, 'Mountain Goat', also runs half and full-day tours in mini-buses equipped with cycle racks designed to get people out of cars and big coaches and onto the network of bike trails. Other local businesses have developed their own schemes as a result of the increased awareness of responsible tourism in the area. Derwentwater Hotel adds a voluntary £1.00 levy to guest bills which goes towards maintaining an important local pathway. The hotel has also introduced new habitats to its sixteen acres of grounds in order to attract wildlife and plants. The Lake District Tourism and Conservation Partnership operates a similar eco-tax where visitors are asked to contribute between £1 and £10 towards local conservation projects. So far they have raised half a million pounds in donations through 170 accredited businesses. As well as the donation scheme the Partnership publishes a holiday guide with a list of shops, accommodation and activities in the area that comply with responsible tourism criteria.

In Lancashire companies have been given advice on how to operate more responsibly and grants to help achieve it. In return they are awarded a 'Green Lantern' standard and promoted to visitors as responsible tourism business. South East Cornwall has a similar scheme where businesses recognised as being responsible receive a 'Green Acorn' award. The logo is displayed on the Tourism Authority's literature and website so visitors can easily identify them. South Hams in Devon runs a green business club where small businesses club together to share responsible tourism information and share bulk buying discounts for green products such as detergent. A recent survey carried out by Visit, a European green tourism accreditation organisation, revealed that companies in the South Hams Green Tourism Business scheme use less energy and water per guest night than any of the other European schemes. Their businesses are rated gold, silver or bronze according to their level of responsible practice.

One of their gold award winners is Beeson Farm Holiday Cottages; a collection of 5 self-catering units in Victorian barns refurbished using traditional techniques and building materials. Beeson employ a recycling policy, use energy efficient appliances and have established a nature reserve. They also provide visitors with information packs about local walks, public transport and the wildlife that can be found in the surrounding Area of Outstanding Natural Beauty. As the accommodation is self-catering, the farm sells its own organic fruit and vegetables and other local produce.

If self-catering isn't for you then Strattons Hotel in Swaffham, Norfolk, may be a more attractive option. This family-owned converted Queen Anne Villa has won several awards for the quality of its service and its dedication to pursuing responsible travel practices. They run a comprehensive recycling scheme and their menu includes locally produced seasonal organic food. All eggs come from their own free-range

chickens that are fed on the organic waste from the kitchen. The hens then do their bit by producing manure that fertilises the trees in the orchard.

Strattons also tries to educate their guests about responsible practices by explaining why they employ their policies and how effective they are. They found that putting miniature cosmetics bottles in the bathroom was not environmentally sound as most were thrown out half full. Now they use dispensers with notes to guests explaining that the change is not a drop in standards but a reduction in landfill.

Towing a caravan may not mean economical motoring, but the Caravan Club claims it is responsible tourism once you arrive. They conducted research that showed families on caravan holidays spend on average £25 per family per day with local businesses, that amounts to over £82 million spent in England's rural economies. The Club has also employed ecologists to carry out biodiversity audits of caravan parks to identify what animals, birds and plants are present and how these and other local species can be encouraged.

If relaxation is not in your travel plans then try a working holiday. The British Trust for Conservation Volunteers runs holidays across the country on projects like dry stone walling, pathway maintenance and habitat management of conservation areas. As the name suggests, World-Wide Opportunities on Organic Farms offers working holidays where in return for your labour on organic farms, smallholdings or gardens you get free organic meals, accommodation and the chance to learn how organic food is produced.

Whatever your requirements for a holiday in England, with the simple things you can do yourself and the growing range of tailored breaks available, there is little excuse not to travel responsibly.

■ The above information was written by Huw Williams and appears on the responsibletravel.com website – visit www.responsibletravel.com or see page 41 for their address details.
© Huw Williams

Ecotourism definitions

Information from Ecotour Directory

Today many different types and definitions of ecotourism exist, however, The International Ecotourism Society (TIES) gives the following definition which has been widely accepted:

'responsible travel to natural areas that conserves the environment and improves the well-being of local people'.

This means that travellers must think and act responsibly in all aspects of their holiday experience in order to minimise their impacts on the environment and local community.

In addition, ecotour companies must hold principles and practices that seek to either preserve or conserve the environment and wildlife whilst protecting and empowering the local people.

The following principles should be followed by everyone who implements and participates in ecotourism activities:

- Minimise impact
- Build environmental and cultural awareness and respect
- Provide positive experiences for both visitors and hosts
- Provide direct financial benefits for conservation
- Provide financial benefits and empowerment for local people
- Raise sensitivity to host countries' political, environmental, and social climate
- Support international human rights and labour agreements.

Further ecotourism definitions

You may have come across some of the following terms that closely relate to ecotourism:

Agro-tourism

This concept is a direct expansion of ecotourism, which encourages visitors to experience agricultural life at first hand. This type of tourism is gathering strong support from small communities as rural people have realised the benefits of sustainable development brought about by similar forms of 'green tourism'. Visitors have the opportunity to work in the fields alongside real farmers and wade knee-deep in the sea with fishermen hauling in their nets.

Travellers must think and act responsibly in all aspects of their holiday experience

---

Community-based tourism

The aims are to enable participation from the local community in the development and operations of tourism with their consent and support. Another important feature is that a reasonable share of the revenues are enjoyed by the community. This type of tourism also maintains and respects the local culture, heritage and traditions. Often, community-based tourism actually reinforces and sometimes rescues these. Community-based tourism also implies respect and concern for the natural heritage, particularly where the environment is one of the attractions.

Nature tourism

This interlinks with ecotourism; however, it concentrates more on enjoying and respecting the wildlife and the environment without the educational element present in ecotourism.

Pro-poor tourism

This type of tourism is set up in developing countries as a means to improve the local economy for local people. It enhances the linkages between tourism businesses and poor people, so that poverty is reduced and poor people are able to participate more effectively in tourism development. The aims of pro-poor range from increasing local employment to involving local people in the decision-making process. Any type of company can be involved such as a small lodge or a tour operator. The most important factor is not the type of company or the type of tourism, but that poor people receive an increase in the net benefits from tourism.

- The above information is from Ecotour Directory's website – visit www.ecotourdirectory.com for more information.

© *Ecotour Directory*

Sustainable tourism

Information from the Foreign and Commonwealth Office

Before you go

- Travelling with respect for the local culture, tradition and holy places earns you respect. Find out about your destination – take some time before you go to read about the cultural, social, religious and political background of the place and people you are visiting. Your welcome will be warmer if you learn a few simple courtesy phrases in the local language.
- Ensure that your travels are Child Right. Consider asking your tour operator if they have a Responsible or Sustainable Tourism policy that includes a condemnation of child sex tourism. Many tour operators work with the World Tourism Organisation to train their staff on the Code of Conduct for the Protection of Children from Sexual Exploitation in Travel and Tourism. For more information on the Code, which is supported by tourism organisations world-wide who want to take action to protect children from sexual abuse, see ECPAT UK and www.thecode.org.
- Read a good guidebook and talk to your travel agent or tour operator about your destination and any possible risks. Visit the national tourism board's website for the country you are visiting.
- Check the FCO Travel Advice available online or by calling 0870 606 0290. The world is an unpredictable place and you need to know about risks to your personal safety and security and trouble spots to avoid. Our travel advice is updated regularly.
- Get adequate Travel Insurance and make sure it includes comprehensive medical and repatriation cover. Make sure it covers you for all activities, including hazardous sports.
- Plan to stay healthy. Ask your travel agent about medical facilities in the country you are visiting and check with your GP at least six weeks before you travel to see if you need to take any extra health precautions (e.g. vaccinations).
- Consider asking your tour operator about their sustainable tourism policy and evidence of the benefits they are bringing to the destinations they visit. When you have finished with your holiday brochures, pass them on to a friend or recycle them.
- If you are thinking of taking a gift for your hosts or people in the country you are visiting then it is best to ask what local people really need before you go. Consider taking something practical.
- Pack appropriately. In many destinations managing waste effectively is expensive or simply not possible. Before you go discard excess waste packaging – for example by removing wrappings from new clothes and toiletries, preferably for recycling. Recycling waste can be difficult and expensive in some destinations.

Be discreet about your views on cultural differences and behave and dress appropriately, particularly when visiting religious sites, markets and rural communities

- Consider offsetting the carbon emissions from your planned flights to minimise global warming. Planting just one tree can offset the carbon dioxide emissions from a short flight. Think about how you might be able to support programmes to help and learn more about the country you plan to visit.

While you are there

- Respect local customs and dress codes. Think about what you wear and how you fit in. Ask your tour operator or local guide if you are unsure about appropriate forms of behaviour, dress codes and how

much to tip. Observe dress codes if you visit religious or cultural sites. Beachwear and public displays of affection may be inappropriate in some areas. Try not to flaunt your (relative) wealth particularly in very poor communities where you are a guest. Remove any expensive jewellery.

- Be discreet about your views on cultural differences and behave and dress appropriately, particularly when visiting religious sites, markets and rural communities. It is always best to err on the side of caution. Behaviour that would be regarded as innocuous elsewhere can lead to serious trouble.

- Ask permission before taking photographs of individuals or of people's homes. Photographing people in some countries without permission can cause offence. It's always best to ask permission first. Remember that you may be expected to pay for the privilege.

- Conserve local resources in your hotel, lodge or camp. Turn down/off heating or air conditioning when not required. Switch off lights when leaving a room and try to turn the television off rather than leaving it on standby. Inform staff if you are happy to re-use towels and bed linen rather than having them replaced daily. Try to use water sparingly.

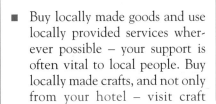

- Buy locally made goods and use locally provided services wherever possible – your support is often vital to local people. Buy locally made crafts, and not only from your hotel – visit craft

centres, stroll the pavements or ask your tour operator/local guide for recommendation about where to shop.

- Help preserve local wildlife and habitats by taking your litter away with you, being sensitive to your surroundings and respecting rules and regulations, such as sticking to footpaths and not standing on coral. Your holiday should not unnecessarily disturb or damage wildlife or habitats. When booking excursions ensure that they respect local fauna and flora. If there is unnecessary disturbance make a complaint to the local operator and your holiday representative.

- Never buy products made from endangered plants or animals. Be aware that buying any wildlife souvenirs or products is highly risky – if in doubt don't buy. Customs throughout the world confiscate illegal souvenirs and in the UK you could face a criminal prosecution and unlimited fines. If you see or hear about any trade in plants or animals that you think might be endangered, call Crimestoppers on 0800 555 111 or the WWF-UK Eyes & Ears hotline on 01483 426111. For more information on endangered species and the WWF-UK Souvenir Alert Campaign for tourists visit www.wwf-uk.org.

- Check that what you are bringing back to the UK is legal. Just because something is on sale in another country does not mean it can be freely brought back to the UK. It is your responsibility to ensure you are not breaking the law. For further information on the regulations on bringing back meat, animal products or plants from outside the EU check with the Department for Environment, Food and Rural Affairs (Defra). Information on banned and restricted goods and your customs allowances is available from HM Customs and Excise online or by calling 0845 010 9000.

- Pay a fair price for the goods and services you buy. Haggle with humour and never aggressively.

Ensure that you get good value but keep a realistic perspective. Consider how (relatively) wealthy many tourists are compared to some local people.

- Think about what happens to your rubbish. Try to use biodegradable products and where appropriate a water filter bottle or purifier to cut down on plastic waste from mineral water containers. Try to reuse plastic bags.

- Be aware of the local laws and attitudes to alcohol. Do not try to import alcohol into a country where it is prohibited – penalties can be severe. Many countries do not allow alcohol to be sold or drunk.

- Be aware of the dangers of becoming involved in drugs overseas. Obey the local laws. In many countries you could be imprisoned for many years, often in grim conditions, fined, or deported for offences that may incur a lesser charge in the UK. You can even receive the death penalty in some countries. We cannot get you out of jail. For information on the environmental impact of the worldwide drugs trade and its economic and social effects on local communities check out the Tourism Concern website.

- Ensure that your travels are Child Right. The Sexual Offences Act 2003 enables British citizens and residents who commit sexual offences against children overseas to be prosecuted in the UK. If you have any information that you think may help the British police enforce these laws you can call Crimestoppers. The calls are completely anonymous. If you are overseas the number is +44 800 555 111. The calls should be made from a landline and you will be charged for the call. If you would like to call Crimestoppers when you return to the UK, the number is 0800 555 111 and you may be eligible for a cash reward.

- The above information is from the Foreign and Commonwealth Office's website which can be found at www.fco.gov.uk

Holidays from hell

Tour operators are profiting from the exploitation of workers and abusive labour conditions are rife in many holiday destinations, says Guyonne James, programme manager at Tourism Concern

Working conditions in the tourism sector are notoriously exploitative, as TSSA (Transport Salaried Staffs' Association) members know only too well. Nowhere is this truer than in developing countries where more and more of us are choosing to take our holidays every year and where poverty and job insecurity are a way of life.

Tourism Concern has done groundbreaking research in five popular holiday destinations – Bali, Mexico, the Dominican Republic, Egypt, and the Canary Islands which has revealed examples of exploitative labour conditions. These include over-dependency on tips, long working hours, unpaid overtime, stress, lack of secure contracts, poor training and almost no promotion opportunity for locally employed people. Research also found that tour operators often use their considerable purchasing power to force down prices in much the same way as supermarkets do when imposing price cuts on farmers. The result is invariably cost-cutting and longer hours for the lowest paid workers. Those who suffer most are the socially weaker and less skilled staff members, a high proportion of whom are women.

In Egypt, cruise ship workers were expected to sign letters accepting voluntary redundancy alongside their employment contract. Employers leave contracts unsigned, making them liable for a small fine if caught, but invalidating the contract. In the Dominican Republic, workers were lucky to get a contract at all. Laundry workers and cleaners reported that long hours and unpaid overtime were standard practice. They also talked about mandatory AIDS tests for local workers but not for foreign staff. In Mexico you can be paid a bonus for not being a member of a union.

The holiday business is a highly competitive, global industry dominated by large western corporations. Where foreign companies own resorts and hotels, any profits from tourism flow straight back to the rich, industrialised nations. The result is that the people living in many exotic tourist destinations, providing the natural, social and cultural resources that make our holidays so pleasurable, frequently receive either an unfairly low return, or actually suffer because of the environmental, social and cultural impact of tourism.

> *Those who suffer most are the socially weaker and less skilled staff members, a high proportion of whom are women*

Tourism accounts for 10.4 per cent of global GDP and 8.1 per cent of jobs worldwide. The large western corporations that dominate tourism, such as the tour operators, are increasingly able to influence the global market at every level, from the World Trade Organisation rules that govern international trade down to the conditions of workers in the hotels we visit. So far they have been more focused on the World Trade Organisation rules that help safeguard their profits than on creating safe, secure, satisfying jobs for the 200 million people who work in the tourism sector globally.

Most of us don't think about what it takes to provide us with our week of relaxation when we book our holiday. Yet our choice of holiday could be contributing to hardship and loss of livelihood for the local people whose communities we visit. Many hotels are built on prime agricultural land, displacing local farmers; the must-have golf courses and the demand for constant running water are often responsible for depleting the local water supply, and staff in many luxury hotels may be struggling to survive on less than a living wage. This is the hidden underside of tourism that certainly isn't shown in the brochures.

In view of the evidence that abusive employment practices are widespread within the tourism industry, that this abuse is unacknowledged and hidden, Tourism Concern is calling on trade unions to demand that tour operators audit labour standards across the tourism supply chain.

There are some easy and simple things you can do as a holidaymaker to ensure that what you spend supports the local community. Find out what the local social and environmental issues are before you go. Stay in a locally owned hotel, look for guided tours that emphasise local involvement, eat food that is grown locally and buy direct from local tradespeople.

■ The above information is from Tourism Concern – visit their website at www.tourismconcern.org.uk or see page 41 for address details.

© *Tourism Concern 2004*

Sun, sand, sea and sweatshops

Frequently asked questions

1. What is Sun, Sand, Sea and SWEATSHOPS?

Sun, Sand, Sea and SWEATSHOPS is a campaign by Tourism Concern, which demands that tour operators take action to ensure fair and legal working conditions in the tourism industry. Research conducted by Tourism Concern has revealed a catalogue of serious problems facing local workers in the tourism industry, including exploitative labour conditions, over-dependency on tips, long working hours, unpaid overtime, stress, lack of secure contracts, poor training and few promotion opportunities.

2. Aren't people better off having a job in tourism rather than factory work or working in the fields? Or no work at all?

This may be true, but it does not mean that paying people less than a legal wage, keeping them in poverty and denying them their human rights is acceptable. When they work long hours for such little pay that they can't even afford to buy an adequate supply of milk for their family, it is time to take action. Tourism workers should be paid a fair and legal price for the service they provide. The fact that in some parts of the world people are desperate for work is no justification for exploitation.

3. Doesn't tourism help the local economy, which makes local people richer?

Tourism can and should provide local prosperity, particularly for developing countries where they have exotic and scenic locations that are so attractive for holidaymakers. Sadly, in a globalised economy dominated by the rich, industrialised nations this is not what happens. Where foreign companies own resorts and hotels, any profits from tourism flow

TourismConcern
Campaigning for Ethical and Fairly Traded Tourism

straight back to these rich countries. The same applies to much of the wealth created by tourism which goes straight back out of local economies in the form of imported goods such as drinks and foods for hotels and services such as the hotel managers. As a result the communities that provide the natural and cultural resources for our holidays get little in return but suffer the social and environmental degradation that follows.

Tourism workers should be paid a fair and legal price for the service they provide

4. There are so many fair trade campaigns right now. What makes this one important?

Tourism is the world's biggest industry and unless local people are provided access to its benefits, the economies of developing countries, in particular, will continue to remain dependent on the rich, industrialised nations. If workers are not paid a living wage or able to buy local goods at a fair price, the benefits of tourism will never filter through to the local economy and people will continue to live in poverty.

5. Will my holidays be more expensive if tourism workers are paid more?

Possibly – if they were under-priced to start with. Tour operators often use their purchasing power to force down prices in much the same way supermarkets do when imposing price cuts on farmers. The result is cost cutting, with the most vulnerable workers, the laundry workers, the porters and cleaners taking the brunt of these cuts and suffering the most. If it adds a few pounds to our holiday then we will just be paying the full cost of our holiday rather than having someone else pay it for us.

■ The above information is from Tourism Concern – visit their website at www.tourismconcern.org.uk or see page 41 for address details.

© *Tourism Concern*

Tourism and people

Information from People and the Planet

Tourism is now the world's largest employer. It plays a crucial role in world economics and has a significant impact on many people's lives – but this impact has been relatively little studied. It is also hard to quantify less tangible impacts such as the effects of tourism on local cultures. In Thailand, for example, trekkers' desire to try opium in hill-tribe villages has led to addiction among village men who smoke with them. On the positive side, tourism can encourage pride in local traditions and support local arts and crafts.

- **Displacement:** Local communities are sometimes forced off their land for tourism development. In Barbados, most of the west coast is owned by large corporations who have made the beaches private property, causing many Barbadians to be displaced and preventing access to fishing areas. Between 1978 and 1998, the Masai in Kenya lost more than 1.5 million acres to tourism and farming. In 1990, 5,200 residents of Pagan, Burma, were evicted from their homes to make way for tourist development. They were given US$3 compensation each and a patch of infertile land 7km away. As part of a partly EU-funded tourism project, San Bushmen in Botswana were evicted from the Central Kalahari Game Reserve in 2002 and moved to a new location which contained none of the plants that the hunter-gathering San relied upon. They continue to campaign to regain access to their ancestral lands. 2004 has seen the forced displacement of hundreds of indigenous people from the inner states of India, in Chhattisgarh, due to government plans to bring tourism to the area through the development of a national park.
- **Child labour:** The International Labour Organisation estimates that between 13 and 19 million

People & the Planet

children under the age of 18 work in tourism. This amounts to between 10 and 15 per cent of the total worldwide tourism labour force.

- **Handicrafts:** Handicrafts offer an important avenue for women, the poor and indigenous communities to earn income from tourism. A 1990 study by Rashtriya Bank in Nepal found that 14.7 per cent of tourist spending went on shopping, mainly for handicrafts.
- **Distorting local economies:** Tour guides and drivers in Bali can earn between US$400 and US$500 per month, compared with a teacher's monthly salary of US$100-150.
- **Sex tourism:** The Thai ministry of public health recorded 65,000 sex workers in 1997, but ILO cites unofficial figures of 200,000 to 300,000. It has been estimated that there are as many as 250,000 children (under-18s) in Thailand, and up to 400,000 in India, working in the sex tourism industry (ECPAT). In a study of 100 schoolchildren in Kalutara, Sri Lanka, 86 had their first sexual experience aged 12 or 13 – the majority with a foreign tourist.

Working conditions

Many jobs in tourism are low-paid with long, unsociable hours.

- Porters in Nepal, a country which in the past has heavily relied on income generated from trekking, typically earn £2-3 a day. Most of the estimated 100,000 porters in the country are employed on a casual basis, while the recent Maoist insurgency has caused tourism to plummet, proving devastating to their work. Porters

die every year due to the effects of altitude and inadequate clothing. In a study of Nepalese porters, 45 per cent had experienced medical problems on treks. The International Porter Protection Group (ippg.org) and Tourism Concern (tourismconcern.org.uk) campaign for better conditions for porters. Porters in Tanzania have launched a union to fight against similar injustices (kilimanjaro-union.com), while the porters working on the Inca Trail are being helped by campaign group the Inka Porter Project (peruweb.org/porters).

- A survey by the Association of British Travel Agents (Travel Industry Rewards Survey, 1999) found workers in the UK tourist industry earned up to 22 per cent less than the national average. Only 65 per cent of employees said they were offered a company pension scheme, compared to the UK average of 95 per cent.

Leakage

Leakage means income from tourism that leaves the destination country. The World Bank estimates that 55 per cent of international tourism income in the South leaves the country via foreign-owned airlines, hotels and tour operators, or payments for imported food, drink and supplies. Studies in individual

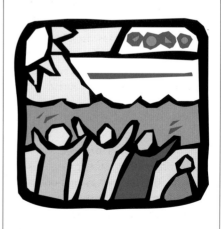

countries have put the figure for leakage even higher – 75 per cent in the Caribbean (DBSA) but as little as 25 per cent for large economies such as India.

- A 1993 study by the World Resources Institute in the Anna-purna region of Nepal found that only 10 per cent of the cost of visitors' holidays remained in the local area.
- Two-thirds of the income from tourism in the Mediterranean – the world's largest tourist destin-ation – returned to less than 10 tour operators from northern Europe (WWF).
- In 1996, a survey found that 57 per cent of Costa Rica's hotels and resorts were foreign-owned, despite laws prohibiting foreign-owned companies from owning coastal properties (Anne Becher, quoted in Honey). In Indonesia in 1997, 90 per cent of 4-star hotels were foreign-owned.

Tourism and gender

Globally, 46 per cent of the tourism workforce are women, compared to an average of 34-40 per cent for the world's workforce as a whole. On average, women working in tourism earn 79 per cent of what men earn, and work 89 per cent of the hours men work – i.e. they are paid less and are more likely to be part-time. Women are much less likely than men to be found in managerial positions and tend to be found in the hotel, catering and restaurant sectors (Gender & Tourism: Women's Employment and Participation in Tourism, UNED-UK Project Report, 1999).

This information was compiled by Mark Mann, author of *The Gringo Trail* and Tourism Concern's *Community Tourism Guide*.

- The above information is re-printed with kind permission from Planet 21, an independent charity providing a well-illustrated educa-tional website on sixteen key themes linking people and the environment – for more information please visit www.peopleandplanet.net or see page 41 for their address details.

© *Planet 21*

Rural community-based tourism

A portal to living cultures

In the age of globalisation, tourism is spreading beyond traditional tourist destinations. In Latin America, a number of small communities are taking up the challenge and seizing the opportunity to improve their conditions of life in ways that respect their heritage.

GENEVA – A journey to the heart of the Mayan forest, to a river inhabited by caimans and piranhas, or to a small, tranquil island, can begin without even leaving home: the traveller has only to visit the 'Redturs' Internet site where more than 100 small communities in six Latin American countries present their natural and cultural attractions and explain to alternative tourists how to get there.

This 'Portal of Living Cultures' is no tourist guidebook but the virtual headquarters of a project run by the International Labour Organisa-tion (ILO) to support indigenous and rural communities in their efforts to create decent jobs and develop healthy economies in ways that protect their cultural heritage and natural resources.

Large numbers of tourists mean opportunities to generate income from tourism. According to figures published by the World Tourism Organisation, some 700 million people travelled abroad in 2003, and the number is expected to grow to 1.6 billion by 2020.

'Globalisation offers opportunities but also creates strong competitive pressures and demands high levels of innovation and specialisation', warns Carlos Maldonado, an ILO expert in charge of the Redturs project which currently includes communities in Bolivia, Brazil, Costa Rica, Ecua-dor, Guatemala and Peru. 'The problem is that many of these small communities are facing a new market with serious structural constraints.'

Redturs, which started up in 2001, this year assumed the functions of technical secretariat of a Sustainable Development Network which aims to facilitate exchanges of inform-ation, spread promotional and market experience, allow sharing of legal and managerial knowledge and provide access to enterprise develop-ment services. The objective is to develop the capacities of the com-munities so that they can benefit from the new tourist flows.

The last meeting of representatives of the small communities involved in the Network, at the end of 2003 in Costa Rica, highlighted the importance of the communities concerned taking up the challenge of providing tourist services themselves. In the Declaration signed in San José, they affirm that 'We refuse to sell or let our land to persons who are not from our communities.'

'We want to ensure that our own communities are the ones in charge of planning, operating, monitoring and developing tourism', according to Rodrigo Flores, President of the Plurinational Federation of Community Tourism of Ecuador (FEPTCE), one of the Redturs participating organisations.

Carlos Maldonado explained that for the community representatives, 'equitable distribution of the revenues that may be generated by tourism is fundamental'.

For Redturs, however, heritage conservation is also a central objective. The San José Declaration makes this clear, and the representatives of the six countries have agreed that whatever the potential economic benefits of a project, it may be halted if it entails 'a burden for our people, our culture and the environment'.

Redturs maintains that in the light of the unprecedented demand for nature tourism and encounters with local cultures, it is vital to aim for a form of tourism that is sustainable, economically viable, environmentally responsible and based on social solidarity. One of the project's fundamental objectives is to create opportunities for decent employment for women and men in these communities, which are often located in remote areas where development opportunities are few.

A virtual trip through the site's 'For the Tourist' section shows the sort of trips on offer.

The trip 'Jungle and piranha fishing with the Huaorani' in Ecuador involves a six-hour journey from Quito overland and by river to an area of humid tropical forest. The trip is operated by Jungle Tour, a small enterprise that has signed an agreement with the local community to promote tourist projects and conservation.

Totally different conditions prevail on the Old Providence and Saint Catalina Islands in Colombia, which offer mountainous landscapes, a coral reef, folklore and small family-run hotels on the Caribbean coast. Trips are run by ECOASTUR, an association embracing hotels, travel agencies and restaurants in these communities that have chosen to join forces 'in order to be able to take decisions independently and make a real difference in the areas of environment and culture'.

According to figures published by the World Tourism Organization, some 700 million people travelled abroad in 2003, and the number is expected to grow to 1.6 billion by 2020

In Livingston, Guatemala, the NGO Ak'Tenamit proposes a trip of several hours from the capital overland and by river to the Tatín and Quehueche region in the heart of the tropical Caribbean rain forest. Working with 30 Q'echi'es Mayan communities, it has begun over the last three years to involve them in providing tourist services as an alternative source of income.

'We are not talking about ecotourism but about something that is both more varied and more specific', according to Maldonado. Nature is a vital element, but the most important aspect is cultural exchange: 'We prefer to call it rural community-based tourism, a term which can encompass ethnotourism, agrotourism, adventure tourism, as well as history and nature tourism, or mystic tourism.'

In 2004 the ILO obtained the first international technical cooperation funds to promote this project. Redturs will now seek to consolidate local and national networks and support promotional and marketing activities. One plan is to establish a 'brand label' certifying the authenticity of community-based tourism projects – that is, tourism based on solidarity, cooperation, respect for life and the sustainable exploitation of ecosystems.

'Redturs' (Sustainable Tourism Network) online can be visited via its 'Portal of Living Cultures' at: www.redturs.org.

■ The above information is from the International Labour Organization – visit www.ilo.org for more or see page 41 for address details.

© *International Labour Organization*

Prevention through awareness

Campaigning on child sex tourism: a market research project

The Issue: child sex tourism

Child sex tourism (CST) is the sexual exploitation of children by adults who travel from their own country to another usually less developed country and engage in sexual activities with the children there.[1] It is often referred to as the commercial sexual exploitation of children (CSEC) in tourism. CSEC includes prostitution, pornography and the trafficking and sale of children. CST is a form of child prostitution, an activity defined as the use of children for sexual gratification by adults for remuneration in cash or kind to the child, or a third party. Sometimes this is organised by an intermediary such as a boyfriend, pimp, family member, neighbour, employer or teacher and may not always involve an exchange of money. It can also include 'in kind' payments such as gifts, food or shelter. According to UNICEF,[2] an estimated one million children enter the commercial sex trade every year around the world.

The extent of the problem of CST is hard to quantify due to the illegal and often hidden nature of the crime. However, a survey carried out by the World Tourism Organization's Child Prostitution Watch recorded cases of CST from 68 countries, either as

sending or receiving countries.[3] There are 64 ECPAT groups working on the issue worldwide which also indicates the extent to which CST is an issue. Extensive research by Julia O'Connell Davidson and Jackie Sanchez Taylor[4] also confirms that it is a very real problem on a global scale. They conducted fieldwork in Costa Rica, Cuba, Dominican Republic, Goa, South Africa and Thailand involving interviews with child sex tourists, a number of whom were British. It is difficult to ascertain the actual numbers of British tourists involved as the nature of the crime means most go undetected. However, the British do account for a substantial percentage of international tourist arrivals worldwide[5] and their involvement cannot be underestimated.

Legal framework

The United Nations Convention on the Rights of the Child (UNCRC, 1989)[6] states that any person under the age of 18 is considered a child and should be protected against any form of sexual exploitation (Article 34). 192 countries, including the UK, have adopted the UNCRC and have agreed to take all appropriate national, bilateral and multilateral measures to protect children from all forms of sexual exploitation and sexual abuse. UN conventions are legally binding.

Differing, and lower, ages of consent are often cited as a defence for child sex abuse overseas. However, it is important to note that it is

illegal to pay for the sexual services of a child in most countries of the world and in the UK, Costa Rica, the Gambia and Thailand the age stipulation is defined as under 18 years.[7]

In the UK it is illegal to engage in prostitution with a person under the age of 18.[8] It is also illegal for UK citizens and residents to engage in sexual activity with children overseas, and extra territorial legislation[9] exists making it possible for a British citizen to be prosecuted in the UK for an offence committed abroad. Additionally, convicted child sex offenders are subject to certain requirements, one of which is having to notify the police whenever they intend to travel overseas for three days or more. The police can, and do, pass this information to other jurisdictions where there is a risk that the offender may offend whilst overseas. Recent legislation in the UK has also introduced a Foreign Travel Order which enables the courts to prohibit a child sex offender from travelling to particular countries or regions, in order to protect children overseas from serious sexual harm.

In practice there have been very few convictions to date in the UK[10] under extra-territorial legislation. This is due to a number of inhibiting factors such as the difficulty in gathering evidence, co-operation of local police forces, difficulty in locating witnesses, or the practicalities of bringing children to the UK to give evidence. Ideally, it is preferable if a person is brought to justice in the country where the offence took place and serves a sentence there. There is a greater impact on offenders if they know they can be arrested in the country and be subject to foreign legislation and sentencing. It also provides an effective warning to other potential offenders if they know police are vigilant. For the country itself, it shows a determination and willingness to prevent CST, not only to other countries and tourists, but also to those involved in the sex trade in that country, including the victims, instigators and perpetrators.

The collaboration on this research project of UK law enforcement stakeholders such as Crimestoppers and NCIS, has been beneficial to researching further into the issue of intelligence gathering on travelling UK child sex offenders. Currently it is difficult to gain an accurate picture of the situation due to the transitory nature of the crime. Offences may be committed whilst a person is on holiday for a short time and then returns home, hence making it difficult to make arrests. Added to which is the identified displacement phenomenon when countries renowned for this activity enact strong law enforcement measures, only for offenders to travel to other countries with weak legal provisions. It would therefore be beneficial for reports to be made in respect of UK travellers to a UK-based agency in order to build up an accurate picture of this activity, in terms of locations and types of people involved. Part of the research has therefore been concerned with establishing whether UK tourists would be willing to a) report and b) use the Crimestoppers number. This would assist UK law enforcement in working together with overseas agencies.

The advantage for UK citizens, whether they are travellers or tour representatives working in the destination, of reporting to a UK-based hotline are numerous. This type of reporting process maintains the anonymity of the reportee and would be English-speaking, therefore reducing the apprehension experienced if reporting to local police authorities. It takes less time and would avoid them having to get involved with the local legal process. The following section analysing the market research data indicates that this could indeed be a viable method that could be used in the process of crime prevention.

Awareness of child sex tourism

All of the respondents were aware of CST with 54% having seen, heard or read a lot about it and 46% not knowing much about it. It is clear therefore that CST can be an issue for customers but it is significant that some felt ill informed about the subject and this could impact on their confidence in reporting an incident.

They had largely gained their awareness through the media in the UK (TV news and documentaries or newspapers) and from personal observation whilst travelling. Countries where CST had been observed ranged from countries across the world with Brazil, Costa Rica, Morocco, Tunisia, Czech Republic, Thailand, Vietnam and Goa all being cited.

Differing, and lower, ages of consent are often cited as a defence for child sex abuse overseas

---

In answer to the question 'How acceptable do you think CST is?' across specified age groups, the following results were recorded: between the ages of 0-10 years 100% said it was unacceptable; between 11-14 years 87% said it was unacceptable and for the 15- to 18-year-old category 67% said it was unacceptable. One respondent was quoted as saying: 'I think one of the main problems is the different ages of consent and what is considered acceptable in their own culture.'

As discussed in the introduction, confusion over ages of consent and differing cultural values are often mentioned and should perhaps therefore be a consideration for the information included in awareness-raising materials.

References
1 ECPAT UK definition
2 UNICEF (2003) 'Faces of Exploitation'. End Child Exploitation Campaign.
3 Group Développement (2001) 'Child Sex Tourism Action Survey'. ECPAT International.
4 ECPAT theme papers for the 1st World Congress (1996).
5 http://www.world-tourism.org/market_research/facts/barometer/january2004.pdf
6 http://www.unicef.org/crc/crc.htm
7 http://www.interpol.int/Public/Children/SexualAbuse/NationalLaws
8 Sexual Offences Act 2003, Part 1, Section 47.
9 Sexual Offences Act 2003, Schedule 2, Section 72.
10 Three

■ This information is an extract from the document 'Prevention through Awareness' – to view the full text, visit www.ecpat.org.uk, or see page 41 for address details.

Picking up the bill

Information from Discovery Initiatives

by Julian Matthews
Founder Director

A great tourism dilemma was graphically illustrated to me just a few weeks ago whilst talking to the amiable governor of a Mongolian soum, the equivalent of an English parish, when he was delighting in the fact that he had just spent $1000 to repair some roads used by tourists to visit a remote Tsaatan reindeer people. This when the governor himself hadn't been paid since February!

'Do you receive much money from tourism?' I said bewildered, knowing that few tourists visit the area.

'None, but we want more like yours.'

So here my hosts were picking up a huge bill on our behalf, and one which will never provide the benefits he believed they could supply.

Tourism carries a heavy cost. A cost wrapped in a thick disguise, trapped in a host's dilemma but sadly hidden in the exclusions clauses that are the ultimate price of our 'once in a lifetime' holiday or more and more these days our once-a-year holiday. How often I have heard developing countries' tourist planners, governments and tour operators wheel out the old chestnuts of creating jobs, bringing in foreign currency and providing much needed development. This is all too seldom the case as it's too often planned from the top not the bottom and because the real costs are wrapped not in the price of your holiday but in the monetary and often high social and cultural cost to your hosts.

So where is all the money that I am spending going to? Often as little as 10p in every pound you are spending on your holiday goes into the country visited. In fact cruise ships spend as little as 3p per person in every port they visit in the Caribbean. Certainly not worth building a harbour for them!

Furthermore, travel to some countries, most especially the less well-off regions in Africa, Asia and South America, is actually costing your hosts money! In fact a considerable sum. Recent Department for International Development research, in a publication entitled *Changing Nature Tourism*, concludes that a visit to Gonarezhou National park in Zimbabwe will cost your hosts US$15.78 (based on the correct assumption that the park provides no direct benefits to its local inhabitants). Yes, those very same lovely smiley Shaangan people you wave at on your way there – that's about £10 to you or I, but a fortune to them. In India the locals will each pay you $2 to visit the famous sanctuary of Keoladeo or in Indonesia a visit to the Komodo Dragons will cost your hosts $13.40. So apart from your hosts being hospitable they are also picking up the bill. Add to this what each of them also pays us in interest payments on their government's colossal debts that we have so generously lent their often inept or corrupt bureaucracies.

So where are the shock troops of the tourism lobby baying for holiday chiefs' blood, blocking entrances to new resorts on unspoilt islands, exposing exploitative companies or lobbying outside Parliament for a fairer trade? Are they all on holiday too?

In fact with a little creativity, a lot more thought and not a little change of attitude, we can change this equation. It's too often forgotten that travel is a service and not a product, and services do not require much, if any, capital and can be 'recycled' simply and often. For example, tourism can provide extraordinary opportunities for low cost locally-owned businesses to flourish through much more than just the ubiquitous souvenirs and low grade employment. Resorts and lodges can buy local food produce, purchase local building materials, make its own furniture, use local transport, provide guiding services, set up alternative attractions or experiences and provide uniforms to mention just a few.

I believe, as the environmentalist Sir Crispin Tickell once illustrated, that conventional attitudes never change till some suitable disaster catches the public imagination, and the facts are laid bare. It's happening with the food industry today; oil spills in Nigeria galvanised the oil industry and dishonest practice shook the banking and insurance sector. The result is positive – our collective consciousness has had profound effects on how these industries see themselves and how they not only present their products but how they get to it in the first place. The consumer suddenly becomes the king!

So what sort of disaster do we need before we can hope to galvanise collective consciousness? The Maldives to sink under the weight of beer bottles, the Serengeti National Park to be turned into a 4-wheel-drive car park or an entrepreneurial Jamaican buying Brighton beach and banning Brightonians from bathing there, with a bold notice to his foreign visitors that says 'Venture out of this beach at your own risk!'

Try this simple test for yourself next time you buy a safari holiday and watch the sales pitch falter. Does the lodge you are staying in employ local people and train them for other than just menial labour? Does it buy

local food produce, is it a joint venture with local communities, does it help fund schools, small business or community projects, sell local artefacts or does it support conservation programmes? If not – try and find some lodge that does! The opportunity to trade with you is what most of the local people, local communities and developing countries need; fairer trade that allows them to benefit from your visit – not pay for it. International aid is absolutely no substitute for the integrity and the respect that your host derives from earning his own crust to support his children.

So let the money you used on your holiday this year be your shield of truth and your sword of justice, and your reward will be returned many times over in experiences that go beyond the normal and conventional. I implore you to use your money wisely and to think just a little about where it might end up, whether you are spending a lot or just a little. Ask a lot about where it goes both before you buy your holiday abroad and again while you are there.

You will be surprised how quickly things will change if enough of us do it.

■ Information from Discovery Initiatives – visit their website at www.discoveryinitiatives.co.uk or see page 41 for their contact details.
© Discovery Initiatives

Sustainable tourism and ecotourism

Various terms attempt to describe tourism that is low-impact, good for the environment and for local communities

Environment-centred definitions

The US-based Ecotourism Society defines ecotourism as 'responsible travel to natural areas that conserves the environment and improves the well-being of local people'. It is usually understood as involving small-group travel.

Nature tourism – the simple visiting and viewing of nature, sometimes disparagingly dubbed 'ecotourism lite' – is not necessarily sustainable. Indeed, tourism to fragile natural destinations can do considerable damage if not carefully managed.

Sustainable tourism is a broader concept than ecotourism. It means any tourism – including urban tourism and mainstream (resort) tourism – that does not degrade the environment.

People-centred definitions

Pro-poor tourism (see the website www.propoortourism.org.uk) means tour-ism that benefits poor people in tourist destinations. The UK-based NGO Tourism Concern is working towards a definition of fair-trade tourism that applies the precepts of fair trade (fair wages, shares of profits) to tourism.

Community tourism (or community-based tourism) denotes tourism where small local communities – typically rural villages in the South – benefit and are involved in the management and decision-making process.

All-embracing terms

Loose terms like alternative, responsible and ethical tourism embrace both environmental and human concerns, but tend to be hard to define in any precise way.

The ecotourism sector

■ 'Wildlife tourism' accounts for an estimated 20 per cent of international tourism.

■ Tourism earned Kenya US$297 million in 2002. It is the country's leading source of foreign exchange, generating a third of the country's foreign currency earnings. The Kenya Wildlife Service estimates that 80 per cent of visitors to Kenya come to see wildlife.

■ The Himalayan Kingdom of Bhutan practises a policy of 'high-value, low-volume' tourism and accepted only 6,000 visitors in 2002, at a cost of US$250 each per day.

■ In 1993, the World Resources Institute estimated countries in the South earned US$30 billion a year from ecotourism.

■ Between 1980 and 1995, visitors to seven 'ecotourism destination' countries with high levels of biodiversity in the South (Brazil, Indonesia, Malaysia, Mexico, Philippines, South Africa, Thailand) rose 242 per cent, from 19.5 million to 47.2 million (WTO).

■ A 1992 survey estimated that 7 per cent (8 million) of US travellers had taken at least one 'ecotourism' holiday. In a 1994 study, 77 per cent of North American tourists had taken a holiday involving nature and the outdoors. The Ecotourism Society estimates that 30 per cent of US tourists can be classed as 'wildlife-related tourists'.

■ In 1996, 219 US companies offered 'ecotours' to the South. However, various commentators estimated that only between 25 and 40 of these were offering 'genuine' sustainable ecotourism (Honey).

Funding bodies

■ International institutions: In the decade up to 1979, the World Bank operated a special tourism department. This backed 24 projects in 18 countries, with a total investment of US$1.5

billion. By 1993, the Asian Development Bank had given £2.12 million to tourism projects. The European Bank for Reconstruction and Redevelopment gave US$12 million towards a hotel development in Albania. By 1996, the World Bank's International Finance Corporation (IFC) had invested in over 100 tourism ventures, providing loans and equity investment of more than US$600 million. Such loans are almost entirely for large mega-developments, such as Cancun in Mexico. Projects supported by the IFC, for instance, usually range from US$5 million to US$150 million (IFC: Tourism Sector Review, 1995).

- Conservation organisations: The three large NGOs that have funded tourism projects are WWF, The Nature Conservancy and Conservation International.

Sustainable tourism: the industry approach

In 1996, the WTTC and WTO published a report called *Local Agenda 21 for the Travel and Tourism Industry* – the industry response to the 1992 Rio Earth Summit's Agenda 21, calling for sustainable development. The report sees tourism developing within the economic framework of NAFTA, GATS and similar 'free trade' agreements.

This means opposing government taxation and (environmental) regulation and removing restrictions on imports and foreign ownership of hotels and companies, thus relying on enlightened corporate self-interest and market forces to move tourism towards sustainability. According to the WTTC's Millennium Vision: 'The environmental policy agenda should focus on [the industry's] self-improvement, incentives, and light-handed regulation as the preferred approach.'

- In 1997, the WTTC successfully opposed a UN proposal for a tax on air travel to fund environmental protection.
- A 2000 survey by WWF claimed that Green Globe, the WTTC-backed environmental cert-

ification scheme, allowed 500 companies to use its logo, although only about 60 of these actually met the criteria involved. In 1995, a fake travel business set up by a TV company (World Television News) was given the right to display a Green Globe symbol for US$200, simply by sending in an application form (Honey).

- This information was compiled by Mark Mann, author of *The Gringo Trail* and *Tourism Concern's Community Tourism Guide*. Planet 21 is an independent charity providing a well-illustrated educational website on sixteen key themes linking people and the environment. See page 41 for their address details or visit www.peopleandplanet.net.

© Planet 21

What are you really bringing back with you?

Think twice before you buy souvenirs and help protect endangered species

Millions of people fly out of the UK each summer in search of sun and relaxation. And many thousands come home with illegal souvenirs made from animal parts – often with no idea that they have done anything wrong.

Yet, we are living in the middle of the biggest mass extinction wave since the disappearance of the dinosaurs – and part of the reason for the decline in some species is the massive poaching that goes on to provide the raw materials for tourist trinkets.

The illegal trade in wildlife is estimated to be worth many billions of dollars each year. While a large part of this trade is controlled by criminal gangs, much is also perpetrated by the hundreds of millions of people who go on foreign holidays each year and unwittingly buy souvenirs made from endangered species.

Each year, Customs agents seize thousands of tourist souvenirs made from endangered species, which are protected by the United Nations Convention on International Trade in Endangered Species of Fauna and Flora (CITES). CITES has been signed by more than 165 countries, and regulates trade in about 5,000 species of animals and 25,000 species of plants.

Unfortunately, souvenirs made from endangered species are often very openly sold in foreign resorts, and so it can be hard for tourists to imagine they are doing any harm. In serious cases, however, tourists coming back home with such products in their luggage are risking hefty fines or even jail sentences.

Endangered species items that are commonly on sale include ivory, tortoiseshell, reptile skins, furs and some corals and seashells. It is illegal to bring many of these products into the UK, while others may require complicated permits.

Many people list their destination's beautiful natural environment and wildlife as a top reason for visiting the country. And yet by buying just one shell, piece of coral or ivory, they are helping to destroy the very natural beauty they came to see! IFAW's Think Twice campaign is asking people travelling abroad to err on the side of caution – if you're not sure what an item is made of, or whether it is legal, then don't buy it. Instead, buy souvenirs such as locally-made handicrafts made from non-animal materials.

- The above information is from the International Fund for Animal Welfare – visit www.ifaw.org for more information.

© IFAW

KEY FACTS

■ Leisure is estimated to account for 75 per cent of all international travel. The World Tourism Organisation (WTO) estimated there were 694 million international tourist arrivals in 2003. (page 1)

■ Three-quarters of all international travellers visit a country in either Europe or North America. However, the share of international tourists travelling to Asia and the Pacific rose from just 1 per cent in 1950 to 17.2 per cent in 2003. (page 1)

■ International tourist arrivals increased from 25 million in 1950 to 693 million in 2003, and are predicted to grow to 1.56 billion by 2020 (WTO). (page 2)

■ Going on holiday was the most popular reason for UK residents to go abroad. In 2003, two-thirds of visits made by UK residents were to go on holiday, with a record 41.2 million holidays taken. About half (47 per cent) of these were package holidays. (page 4)

■ In 2004 nearly 28 million international visitors spent £13 billion in the UK. (page 6)

■ Almost two in four (38%) adults had booked a holiday independently in 2003, compared to just one in four (25%) who had booked a package holiday. What is more, the popularity of independent holidays is expected to continue to increase further, with expenditure on these holidays forecast to rise by a massive 78%. (page 8)

■ The new backpackers – or 'global nomads' – are degree educated, have strong opinions about social justice and world peace, and see travel as a culturally valuable stage on life's way. (page 10)

■ Of the 250,000 18- to 24-year-old backpackers leaving the UK over the next six months, one in three will travel without insurance. (page 14)

■ Australia is the number-one destination UK package holidaymakers would most like to visit. (page 15)

■ The Internet is now firmly established as a booking tool for holidays, with 19% of holidaymakers booking their package holiday online in 2004 – six times the number compared to the year 2000. (page 16)

■ 8,010 people visited London from Europe in 2004. (page 16)

■ Tourism has become the main money earner for a third of developing nations, and the primary source of foreign exchange earnings for most of the 49 least developed countries. (page 18)

■ A single passenger on a return London to New York flight produces more carbon dioxide than the average UK motorist does in a year. (page 19)

■ Several regions of England have developed integrated responsible tourism policies. They encourage local businesses to operate more responsibly, promote public transport geared towards tourist routes, implement recycling schemes and support conservation programmes. (page 26)

■ The International Ecotourism Society (TIES) gives the following definition of ecotourism which has been widely accepted: 'responsible travel to natural areas that conserves the environment and improves the well-being of local people'. (page 27)

■ Types of ecotourism include agro-tourism, community-based tourism, nature tourism and pro-poor tourism. (page 27)

■ Just because something is on sale in another country does not mean it can be freely brought back to the UK. It is your responsibility to ensure you are not breaking the law. (page 29)

■ Tourism accounts for 10.4 per cent of global GDP and 8.1 per cent of jobs worldwide. (page 30)

■ Where foreign companies own resorts and hotels, any profits from tourism flow straight back to these rich countries. (page 31)

■ Leakage means income from tourism that leaves the destination country. The World Bank estimates that 55 per cent of international tourism income in the South leaves the country via foreign-owned airlines, hotels and tour operators, or payments for imported food, drink and supplies. (page 32)

■ Differing, and lower, ages of consent are often cited as a defence for child sex abuse overseas. However, it is important to note that it is illegal to pay for the sexual services of a child in most countries of the world and in the UK, Costa Rica, the Gambia and Thailand the age stipulation is defined as under 18 years. (page 35)

■ Often as little as 10p in every pound you are spending on your holiday goes into the country visited. In fact cruise ships spend as little as 3p per person in every port they visit in the Caribbean. (page 37)

■ Sustainable tourism is a broader concept than ecotourism. It means any tourism that does not degrade the environment. (page 38)

ADDITIONAL RESOURCES

You might like to contact the following organisations for further information. Due to the increasing cost of postage, many organisations cannot respond to enquiries unless they receive a stamped, addressed envelope.

Association of British Travel Agents (ABTA)
68-71 Newman Street
LONDON
W1T 3AH
Tel: 020 7637 2444
Fax: 020 7637 0713
Email: abta@abta.co.uk
Website: www.abta.com
The Association of British Travel Agents is the UK's Premier Trade Association for Tour Operators and Travel Agents. ABTA's 800 tour operators and 6700 travel agency offices are responsible for the sale of some 80% of UK-sold holidays.

British Tourist Authority (Visit Britain)
Thames Tower
Black's Road
LONDON
W6 9EL
Tel: 020 8846 9000
Email: blvcinfo@visitbritain.org
Website: www.visitbritain.com
VisitBritain markets Britain to the rest of the world and England to the British, building the value of tourism throughout Britain and throughout the year by creating world-class destination brands and marketing campaigns. It also builds partnerships with – and provides insights to – other organisations that have a stake in British and English tourism.

Discovery Initiatives
The Travel House
51 Castle Street
CIRENCESTER
Gloucestershire GL7 1QD
Tel: 01285 643333
Email: enquiry@discoveryinitiatives.com
Website: www.discoveryinitiatives.com
By working in cooperation with the conservation community we intend to enhance the work of those involved in local conservation projects by linking into the demand for nature travel. Our mission has been to show that it is no longer acceptable for the travel industry to think purely of economic return and profit but to evolve a more rounded approach that recognises environmental and social concerns. Our objective: to challenge the conventional approach to nature or wilderness travel.

ECPAT
328 Phyathai Road
10400 Bangkok
THAILAND
Tel: + 66 2 215 3388
Fax: + 66 2 215 8272
Website: www.earthtimes.org
ECPAT (the campaign to End Child Prostitution, Child Pornography And the Trafficking of children) has been instrumental in exposing sexual abuse to the media and placing it on the political agenda.

International Labour Organization (ILO)
Millbank Tower
21-24 Mill Bank
LONDON
SW1P 4QP
Tel: 0207 828 6401
Fax: 0207 233 5925
Email: london@ilo.org
Website: www.ilo.org
The International Labour Organisation is the United Nations agency with global responsibility for work, employment and labour market issues.

Office for National Statistics (ONS)
Zone B1/04
1 Drummond Gate
Pimlico
LONDON
SW1V 2QQ
Tel: 020 7533 5264
Website: www.statistics.gov.uk
Formerly the Office of Population, Censors and Surveys (OPCS). The Office for National Statistics (ONS) is the government department that provides UK statistical and registration services.

Planet 21
60 Twisden Road
LONDON
NW5 1DN
Tel: 020 7485 3136
Email: planet21@totalise.co.uk
Website: www.peopleandplanet.net
peopleandplanet.net provides a global review and Internet gateway into the issues of population, poverty, health, consumption and the environment. It is published by Planet 21, an independent non-profit company and a registered British charity recognised by the United Nations.

Tourism Concern
Stapleton House
277-281 Holloway Road
LONDON
N7 8HN
Tel: 020 7133 3330
Fax: 020 7133 3331
Email: info@tourismconcern.org.uk
Website: www.tourismconcern.org.uk
Tourism Concern is a membership organisation campaigning for ethical and fairly traded tourism.

World Tourism Organization (WTO)
Capitán Haya, 42
28020 Madrid
SPAIN
Tel: 00 34 91 567 81 00
Fax: 00 34 91 571 37 33
Email: infoshop@world-tourism.org
Website: www.world-tourism.org
The World Tourism Organization is the leading international organisation in the field of travel and tourism. It serves as a global forum for tourism policy issues and a practical source of tourism know-how.

INDEX

ACKNOWLEDGEMENTS

The publisher is grateful for permission to reproduce the following material.

While every care has been taken to trace and acknowledge copyright, the publisher tenders its apology for any accidental infringement or where copyright has proved untraceable. The publisher would be pleased to come to a suitable arrangement in any such case with the rightful owner.

Chapter One: Tourism Issues

Global tourism: growing fast, © Planet 21 2004, *International travel increases*, © Crown Copyright is reproduced with the permission of Her Majesty's Stationery Office 2004, *UK travel trends*, © Crown Copyright is reproduced with the permission of Her Majesty's Stationery Office 2005, *UK tourism at all-time high*, © VisitBritain 2005, *Tourism is changing*, © Crown Copyright is reproduced with the permission of Her Majesty's Stationery Office 2005, *Major boost for world tourism*, © World Tourism Organization 2005, *Independent holidays*, © Mintel 2004, *The new seekers*, © Guardian Newspapers Limited 2005, *Passport to fun*, © Crown Copyright is reproduced with the permission of Her Majesty's Stationery Office 2005, *Risky business*, © gapyear.com, *Australia – still top dream holiday spot for Brits*, © ABTA 2004, *Travel agents and Internet bookings*, © ABTA 2004, *Branson promises to send tourists into space by 2007*, © Telegraph Group Limited 2004.

Chapter Two: Responsible Tourism

The good tourist guide, © Richard Hammond, *Are we loving our heritage to death?*, © Guardian Newspapers Limited 2005, *An ecotourism glossary*, © Planet 21, *An even greener and more pleasant land*, © Huw Williams, *Ecotourism definitions*, © Ecotour Directory, *Sustainable tourism*, © Crown Copyright is reproduced with the permission of Her Majesty's Stationery Office, *Holidays from hell*, © Tourism Concern 2004, *Sun, sand, sea and sweatshops*, © Tourism Concern, *Tourism and people*, © Planet 21, *Rural community-based tourism*, © International Labour Organization, *Prevention through awareness*, © ECPAT 2004, *Picking up the bill*, © Discovery Initiatives, *Sustainable tourism and ecotourism*, © Planet 21, *What are you really bringing back with you?*, © IFAW.

Photographs and illustrations:

Pages 1, 21, 28: Angelo Madrid; pages 4, 14, 22, 31, 36: Simon Kneebone; pages 8, 17: Pumpkin House; pages 10, 18, 27: Don Hatcher; pages 13, 24, 34: Bev Aisbett.

Craig Donnellan
Cambridge
September, 2005